Joy by John Galsworthy

A PLAY ON THE LETTER "I". IN THREE ACTS

First Series Plays

John Galsworthy was born at Kingston Upon Thames in Surrey, England, on August 14th 1867 to a wealthy and well established family. His schooling was at Harrow and New College, Oxford before training as a barrister and being called to the bar in 1890. However, Law was not attractive to him and he travelled abroad becoming great friends with the novelist Joseph Conrad, then a first mate on a sailing ship.

In 1895 Galsworthy began an affair with Ada Nemesis Pearson Cooper, the wife of his cousin Major Arthur Galsworthy. The affair was kept a secret for 10 years till she at last divorced and they married on 23 September 1905.

John Galsworthy first published in 1897 with a collection of short stories entitled "The Four Winds". For the next 7 years he published these and all works under his pen name John Sinjohn. It was only upon the death of his father and the publication of "The Island Pharisees" in 1904 that he published as John Galsworthy. In this volume we have Villa Rubein ays and studies. They are the work of a supreme talent at the top of his game. Whilst today he is far more well know as a Nobel Prize winning novelist then he was considered a playwright dealing with social issues and the class system. He was appointed to the Order of Merit in 1929, after earlier turning down a knighthood, and awarded the Nobel Prize in 1932 though he was too ill to attend. John Galsworthy died from a brain tumour at his London home, Grove Lodge, Hampstead on January 31st 1933. In accordance with his will he was cremated at Woking with his ashes then being scattered over the South Downs from an aeroplane.

He is now far better known for his novels, particularly The Forsyte Saga, his trilogy about the eponymous family of the same name. These books, as with many of his other works, deal with social class, upper-middle class lives in particular. Although always sympathetic to his characters, he reveals their insular, snobbish, and somewhat greedy attitudes and suffocating moral codes. He is now viewed as one of the first from the Edwardian era to challenge some of the ideals of society depicted in the literature of Victorian England.

In his writings he campaigns for a variety of causes, including prison reform, women's rights, animal welfare, and the opposition of censorship as well as a recurring theme of an unhappy marriage from the women's side. During World War I he worked in a hospital in France as an orderly after being passed over for military service.

He was appointed to the Order of Merit in 1929, after earlier turning down a knighthood, and awarded the Nobel Prize in 1932 though he was too ill to attend.

John Galsworthy died from a brain tumour at his London home, Grove Lodge, Hampstead on January 31st 1933. In accordance with his will he was cremated at Woking with his ashes then being scattered over the South Downs from an aeroplane.

Index of Contents

PERSONS OF THE PLAY

COLONEL HOPE, R.A., retired
MRS. HOPE, his wife
MISS BEECH, their old governess
LETTY, their daughter
ERNEST BLUNT, her husband
MRS. GWYN, their niece
JOY, her daughter
DICK MERTON, their young friend
HON. MAURICE LEVER, their guest ROSE, their parlour-maid

TIME

The present.

SCENE

The action passes throughout midsummer day on the lawn of Colonel Hope's house, near the Thames above Oxford.

ACT I

The time is morning, and the scene a level lawn, beyond which the river is running amongst fields. A huge old beech tree overshadows everything, in the darkness of whose hollow many things are hidden. A rustic seat encircles it. A low wall clothed in creepers, with two openings, divides this lawn from the flowery approaches to the house. Close to the wall there is a swing. The sky is clear and sunny. **COLONEL HOPE** is seated in a garden-chair, reading a newspaper through pince-nez. He is fifty-five and bald, with drooping grey moustaches and a weather-darkened face. He wears a flannel suit and a hat from Panama; a tennis racquet leans against his chair. **MRS HOPE** comes quickly through the opening of the wall, with roses in her hands. She is going grey; she wears tan gauntlets, and no hat. Her manner is decided, her voice emphatic, as though aware that there is no nonsense in its owner's composition. Screened from sight, **MISS BEECH** is seated behind the hollow tree; and **JOY** is perched on a lower branch hidden by foliage.

MRS HOPE
I told Molly in my letter that she'd have to walk up, Tom.

COLONEL
Walk up in this heat? My dear, why didn't you order Benson's fly?

MRS HOPE
Expense for nothing! Bob can bring up her things in the barrow. I've told Joy I won't have her going down to meet the train. She's so excited about her mother's coming there's no doing anything with her.

COLONEL
No wonder, after two months.

MRS HOPE
Well, she's going home to-morrow; she must just keep herself fresh for the dancing tonight. I'm not going to get people in to dance, and have Joy worn out before they begin.

COLONEL [Dropping his paper.]
I don't like Molly's walking up.

MRS HOPE
A great strong woman like Molly Gwyn! It isn't half a mile.

COLONEL
I don't like it, Nell; it's not hospitable.

MRS HOPE
Rubbish! If you want to throw away money, you must just find some better investment than those wretched 3 per cents. of yours. The greenflies are in my roses already! Did you ever see anything so disgusting? [They bend over the roses they have grown, and lose all sense of everything.] Where's the syringe? I saw you mooning about with it last night, Tom.

COLONEL [Uneasily.]
 Mooning!

[He retires behind his paper. **MRS HOPE** enters the hollow of the tree.

There's an account of that West Australian swindle. Set of ruffians! Listen to this, Nell! "It is understood that amongst the share-holders are large numbers of women, clergymen, and Army officers." How people can be such fools!

[Becoming aware that his absorption is unobserved, he drops his glasses, and reverses his chair towards the tree.]

MRS HOPE [Reappearing with a garden syringe.]

I simply won't have Dick keep his fishing things in the tree; there's a whole potful of disgusting worms. I can't touch them. You must go and take 'em out, Tom.

[In his turn the **COLONEL** enters the hollow of the tree.

MRS HOPE [Personally.]

What on earth's the pleasure of it? I can't see! He never catches anything worth eating.

[The **COLONEL** reappears with a paint pot full of worms; he holds them out abstractedly.

MRS HOPE [Jumping.]

Don't put them near me!

MISS BEECH [From behind the tree.]

Don't hurt the poor creatures.

COLONEL [Turning.]

Hallo, Peachey? What are you doing round there?

[He puts the worms down on the seat.

MRS HOPE

Tom, take the worms off that seat at once!

COLONEL [Somewhat flurried.]

Good gad! I don't know what to do with the beastly worms!

MRS HOPE

It's not my business to look after Dick's worms. Don't put them on the ground. I won't have them anywhere where they can crawl about. [She flicks some greenflies off her roses.]

COLONEL [Looking into the pot as though the worms could tell him where to put them.]

Dash!

MISS BEECH

Give them to me.

MRS HOPE [Relieved.]

Yes, give them to Peachey.

[There comes from round the tree **MISS BEECH**, old-fashioned, barrel-shaped, balloony in the skirts. She takes the paint pot, and sits beside it on the rustic seat.

MISS BEECH

Poor creatures!

MRS HOPE

Well, it's beyond me how you can make pets of worms— wriggling, crawling, horrible things!

[**ROSE**, who is young and comely, in a pale print frock, comes from the house and places letters before her on a silver salver.

[Taking the letters.

What about Miss joy's frock, Rose?

ROSE
Please, 'm, I can't get on with the back without Miss Joy.

MRS HOPE
Well, then you must just find her. I don't know where she is.

ROSE [In a slow, sidelong manner.]
If you please, Mum, I think Miss Joy's up in the—

[She stops, seeing **MISS BEECH** signing to her with both hands.

MRS HOPE [Sharply.]
What is it, Peachey?

MISS BEECH [Selecting a finger.]
Pricked meself!

MRS HOPE
Let's look!

[She bends to look, but **MISS BEECH** places the finger in her mouth.

ROSE [Glancing askance at the **COLONEL**.]
If you please, Mum, it's below the waist; I think I can manage with the dummy.

MRS HOPE
Well, you can try.

[Opening her letter as **ROSE** retires.

Here's Molly about her train.

MISS BEECH
Is there a letter for me?

MRS HOPE
No, Peachey.

MISS BEECH

There never is.

COLONEL
What's that? You got four by the first post.

MISS BEECH
Exceptions!

COLONEL [Looking over his glasses.]
Why! You know, you get 'em every day!

MRS HOPE
Molly says she'll be down by the eleven thirty. [In an injured voice.] She'll be here in half an hour!
[Reading with disapproval from the letter.] "MAURICE LEVER is coming down by the same train to see
Mr. Henty about the Tocopala Gold Mine. Could you give him a bed for the night?"

[Silence, slight but ominous.]

COLONEL [Calling into his aid his sacred hospitality.]
Of course we must give him a bed!

MRS HOPE
Just like a man! What room I should like to know!

COLONEL
Pink.

MRS HOPE
As if Molly wouldn't have the pink!

COLONEL [Ruefully.]
I thought she'd have the blue!

MRS HOPE
You know perfectly well it's full of earwigs, Tom. I killed ten there yesterday morning.

MISS BEECH
Poor creatures!

MRS HOPE
I don't know that I approve of this Mr. Lever's dancing attendance. Molly's only thirty-six.

COLONEL [In a high voice.]
You can't refuse him a bed; I never heard of such a thing.

MRS HOPE [Reading from the letter.]

"This gold mine seems to be a splendid chance. [She glances at the **COLONEL**.] I've put all my spare cash into it. They're issuing some Preference shares now; if Uncle Tom wants an investment"—[She pauses, then in a changed, decided voice]—Well, I suppose I shall have to screw him in somehow.

COLONEL
What's that about gold mines? Gambling nonsense! Molly ought to know my views.

MRS HOPE [Folding the letter away out of her consciousness.]
Oh! your views! This may be a specially good chance.

MISS BEECH
Ahem! Special case!

MRS HOPE [Paying no attention.]
I 'm sick of these 3 per cent. dividends. When you've only got so little money, to put it all into that India Stock, when it might be earning 6 per cent. at least, quite safely! There are ever so many things I want.

COLONEL
There you go!

MRS HOPE
As to Molly, I think it's high time her husband came home to look after her, instead of sticking out there in that hot place. In fact—

[**MISS BEECH** looks up at the tree and exhibits cerebral excitement]

I don't know what Geoff's about; why doesn't he find something in England, where they could live together.

COLONEL
Don't say anything against Molly, Nell!

MRS HOPE
Well, I don't believe in husband and wife being separated. That's not my idea of married life.

[The **COLONEL** whistles quizzically.]

Ah, yes, she's your niece, not mime! Molly's very—

MISS BEECH
Ouch!

[She sucks her finger.]

MRS HOPE
Well, if I couldn't sew at your age, Peachey, without pricking my fingers! Tom, if I have Mr. Lever here, you'll just attend to what I say and look into that mine!

COLONEL
Look into your grandmother! I have n't made a study of geology for nothing. For every ounce you take out of a gold mine, you put an ounce and a half in. Any fool knows that, eh, Peachey?

MISS BEECH
I hate your horrid mines, with all the poor creatures underground.

MRS HOPE
Nonsense, Peachey! As if they'd go there if they did n't want to!

COLONEL
Why don't you read your paper, then you'd see what a lot of wild-cat things there are about.

MRS HOPE [Abstractedly.]
I can't put Ernest and Letty in the blue room, there's only the single bed. Suppose I put Mr. Lever there, and say nothing about the earwigs. I daresay he'll never notice.

COLONEL
Treat a guest like that!

MRS HOPE
Then where am I to put him for goodness sake?

COLONEL
Put him in my dressing-room, I'll turn out.

MRS HOPE
Rubbish, Tom, I won't have you turned out, that's flat. He can have Joy's room, and she can sleep with the earwigs.

JOY [From her hiding-place upon a lower branch of the hollow tree.]
I won't.

[**MRS HOPE** and the **COLONEL** jump.

COLONEL
God bless my soul!

MRS HOPE
You wretched girl! I told you never to climb that tree again. Did you know, Peachey?

[**MISS BEECH** smiles.]

She's always up there, spoiling all her frocks. Come down now, Joy; there's a good child!

JOY
I don't want to sleep with earwigs, Aunt Nell.

MISS BEECH
I'll sleep with the poor creatures.

MRS HOPE [After a pause.]
Well, it would be a mercy if you would for once, Peachey.

COLONEL
Nonsense, I won't have Peachey—

MRS HOPE
Well, who is to sleep there then?

JOY [Coaxingly.]
Let me sleep with Mother, Aunt Nell, do!

MRS HOPE
Litter her up with a great girl like you, as if we'd only one spare room! Tom, see that she comes down—I can't stay here, I must manage something.

[She goes away towards the house.]

COLONEL [Moving to the tree, and looking up.]
You heard what your aunt said?

JOY [Softly.]
Oh, Uncle Tom!

COLONEL
I shall have to come up after you.

JOY
Oh, do, and Peachey too!

COLONEL [Trying to restrain a smile.]
Peachey, you talk to her.

[Without waiting for **MISS BEECH**, however, he proceeds.

What'll your aunt say to me if I don't get you down?

MISS BEECH
Poor creature!

JOY
I don't want to be worried about my frock.

COLONEL [Scratching his bald head.]
Well, I shall catch it.

JOY

Oh, Uncle Tom, your head is so beautiful from here! [Leaning over, she fans it with a leafy twig.]

MISS BEECH

Disrespectful little toad!

COLONEL [Quickly putting on his hat.]

You'll fall out, and a pretty mess that'll make on—[he looks uneasily at the ground]—my lawn!

[A **VOICE** is heard calling "Colonel! Colonel!)"

JOY

There's Dick calling you, Uncle Tom.

[She disappears.

DICK

[Appearing in the opening of the wall.] Ernie's waiting to play you that single, Colonel!

[He disappears.

JOY

Quick, Uncle Tom! Oh! do go, before he finds I 'm up here.

MISS BEECH

Secret little creature!

[The **COLONEL** picks up his racquet, shakes his fist, and goes away.

JOY [Calmly.]

I'm coming down now, Peachey.

[Climbing down.]

Look out! I'm dropping on your head.

MISS BEECH [Unmoved.]

Don't hurt yourself!

[**JOY** drops on the rustic seat and rubs her shin. Told you so!

[She hunts in a little bag for plaster.

Let's see!

JOY [Seeing the worms.]

Ugh!

MISS BEECH
What's the matter with the poor creatures?

JOY
They're so wriggly!

[She backs away and sits down in the swing. She is just seventeen, light and slim, brown-haired, fresh-coloured, and grey-eyed; her white frock reaches to her ankles, she wears a sunbonnet.

Peachey, how long were you Mother's governess.

MISS BEECH
Five years.

JOY
Was she as bad to teach as me?

MISS BEECH
Worse!

[**JOY** claps her hands.

She was the worst girl I ever taught.

JOY
Then you weren't fond of her?

MISS BEECH
Oh! yes, I was.

JOY
Fonder than of me?

MISS BEECH
Don't you ask such a lot of questions.

JOY
Peachey, duckie, what was Mother's worst fault?

MISS BEECH
Doing what she knew she oughtn't.

JOY
Was she ever sorry?

MISS BEECH
Yes, but she always went on doin' it.

JOY
I think being sorry 's stupid!

MISS BEECH
Oh, do you?

JOY
It isn't any good. Was Mother revengeful, like me?

MISS BEECH
Ah! Wasn't she?

JOY
And jealous?

MISS BEECH
The most jealous girl I ever saw.

JOY
[Nodding.] I like to be like her.

MISS BEECH [Regarding her intently.]
Yes! you've got all your troubles before you.

JOY
Mother was married at eighteen, wasn't she, Peachey? Was she— was she much in love with Father then?

MISS BEECH [With a sniff.]
About as much as usual.

[She takes the paint pot, and walking round begins to release the worms.

JOY [Indifferently.]
They don't get on now, you know.

MISS BEECH
What d'you mean by that, disrespectful little creature?

JOY [In a hard voice.]
They haven't ever since I've known them. Miss Beech.

[Looks at her, and turns away again.

Don't talk about such things.

JOY

I suppose you don't know Mr. Lever? [Bitterly.] He's such a cool beast. He never loses his temper.

MISS BEECH
Is that why you don't like him?

JOY
[Frowning.] No—yes—I don't know.

MISS BEECH
Oh! perhaps you do like him?

JOY
I don't; I hate him.

MISS BEECH [Standing still.]
Fie! Naughty Temper!

JOY
Well, so would you! He takes up all Mother's time.

MISS BEECH [In a peculiar voice.]
Oh! does he?

JOY
When he comes I might just as well go to bed. [Passionately.] And now he's chosen to-day to come down here, when I haven't seen her for two months! Why couldn't he come when Mother and I'd gone home. It's simply brutal!

MISS BEECH
But your mother likes him?

JOY [Sullenly.]
I don't want her to like him.

MISS BEECH
[With a long look at Joy.] I see!

JOY
What are you doing, Peachey?

MISS BEECH [Releasing a worm.]
Letting the poor creatures go.

JOY
If I tell Dick he'll never forgive you.

MISS BEECH [Sidling behind the swing and plucking off Joy's sunbonnet. With devilry.]
Ah-h-h! You've done your hair up; so that's why you wouldn't come down!

JOY [Springing up, anal pouting.]
I didn't want any one to see before Mother. You are a pig, Peachey!

MISS BEECH
I thought there was something!

JOY [Twisting round.]
How does it look?

MISS BEECH
I've seen better.

JOY
You tell any one before Mother comes, and see what I do!

MISS BEECH
Well, don't you tell about my worms, then!

JOY
Give me my hat! [Backing hastily towards the tree, and putting her finger to her lips.] Look out! Dick!

MISS BEECH
Oh! dear!

[She sits down on the swing, concealing the paint pot with her feet and skirts.]

JOY [On the rustic seat, and in a violent whisper.]
I hope the worms will crawl up your legs!

[**DICK**, in flannels and a hard straw hat comes in. He is a quiet and cheerful boy of twenty. His eyes are always fixed on joy.]

DICK [Grimacing.]
The Colonel's getting licked. Hallo! Peachey, in the swing?

JOY [Chuckling.]
Swing her, Dick!

MISS BEECH [Quivering with emotion.]
Little creature!

JOY
Swing her!

[**DICK** takes the ropes.

MISS BEECH [Quietly.]

It makes me sick, young man.

DICK [Patting her gently on the back.]
All right, Peachey.

MISS BEECH [Maliciously.]
Could you get me my sewing from the seat? Just behind Joy.

JOY [Leaning her head against the tree.]
If you do, I won't dance with you to-night.

[**DICK** stands paralysed. **MISS BEECH** gets off the swing, picks up the paint pot, and stands concealing it behind her.

JOY
Look what she's got behind her, sly old thing!

MISS BEECH
Oh! dear!

JOY
Dance with her, Dick!

MISS BEECH
If he dare!

JOY
Dance with her, or I won't dance with you to-night.

[She whistles a waltz.

DICK [Desperately.]
Come on then, Peachey. We must.

JOY
Dance, dance!

[**DICK** seizes **MISS BEECH** by the waist. She drops the paint pot. They revolve.

[Convulsed.]
Oh, Peachey, Oh!

[**MISS BEECH** is dropped upon the rustic seat. **DICK** seizes **JOY'S** hands and drags her up.

No, no! I won't!

MISS BEECH [Panting.]
Dance, dance with the poor young man! [She moves her hands.] La la-la-la la-la la la!

[**DICK** and **JOY** dance.]

DICK
By Jove, Joy! You've done your hair up. I say, how jolly! You do look—

JOY [Throwing her hands up to her hair.]
I did n't mean you to see!

DICK [In a hurt voice.]
Oh! didn't you? I'm awfully sorry!

JOY [Flashing round.]
Oh, you old Peachey!

[She looks at the ground, and then again at **DICK**.

MISS BEECH [Sidling round the tree.]
Oh! dear!

JOY [Whispering.]
She's been letting out your worms.

[**MISS BEECH** disappears from view.]

Look!

DICK [Quickly.]
Hang the worms! Joy, promise me the second and fourth and sixth and eighth and tenth and supper, to-night. Promise! Do!

[**JOY** shakes her head.]

It's not much to ask.

JOY
I won't promise anything.

DICK
Why not?

JOY
Because Mother's coming. I won't make any arrangements.

DICK [Tragically.]
It's our last night.

JOY [Scornfully.]

You don't understand!

[Dancing and clasping her hands.

Mother's coming, Mother's coming!

DICK [Violently.]
I wish—Promise, Joy!

JOY [Looking over her shoulder.]
Sly old thing! If you'll pay Peachey out, I'll promise you supper!

MISS BEECH [From behind the tree.]
I hear you.

JOY [Whispering.]
Pay her out, pay her out! She's let out all your worms!

DICK [Looking moodily at the paint pot.]
I say, is it true that Maurice Lever's coming with your mother? I've met him playing cricket, he's rather a good sort.

JOY [Flashing out.]
I hate him.

DICK [Troubled.]
Do you? Why? I thought—I didn't know—if I'd known of course, I'd have—

[He is going to say "hated him too!" But the voices of **ERNEST BLUNT** and the **COLONEL** are heard approaching, in dispute.

JOY
Oh! Dick, hide me, I don't want my hair seen till Mother comes.

[She springs into the hollow tree. The **COLONEL** and **ERNEST** appear in the opening of the wall.]

ERNEST
The ball was out, Colonel.

COLONEL
Nothing of the sort.

ERNEST
A good foot out.

COLONEL
It was not, sir. I saw the chalk fly.

[**ERNEST** is twenty-eight, with a little moustache, and the positive cool voice of a young man who knows that he knows everything. He is perfectly calm.

ERNEST
I was nearer to it than you.

COLONEL [In a high, hot voice.]
I don't care where you were, I hate a fellow who can't keep cool.

MISS BEECH [From behind the hollow tree.]
Fie! Fie!

ERNEST
We're two to one, Letty says the ball was out.

COLONEL
Letty's your wife, she'd say anything.

ERNEST
Well, look here, Colonel, I'll show you the very place it pitched.

COLONEL
Gammon! You've lost your temper, you don't know what you're talking about.

ERNEST [Coolly.]
I suppose you'll admit the rule that one umpires one's own court.

COLONEL [Hotly.]
Certainly not, in this case!

MISS BEECH [From behind the hollow tree.]
Special case!

ERNEST [Moving chin in collar—very coolly.]
Well, of course if you won't play the game!

COLONEL [In a towering passion.]
If you lose your temper like this, I'll never play with you again.

[To **LETTY**, a pretty soul in a linen suit, approaching through the wall.

Do you mean to say that ball was out, Letty?

LETTY
Of course it was, Father.

COLONEL
You say that because he's your husband.

[He sits on the rustic seat.]

If your mother'd been there she'd have backed me up!

LETTY
Mother wants Joy, Dick, about her frock.

DICK
I—I don't know where she is.

MISS BEECH [From behind the hollow tree.]
Ahem!

LETTY
What's the matter, Peachey?

MISS BEECH
Swallowed a fly. Poor creature!

ERNEST [Returning to his point.]
Why I know the ball was out, Colonel, was because it pitched in a line with that arbutus tree.

COLONEL [Rising.]
Arbutus tree! [To his daughter.] Where's your mother?

LETTY
In the blue room, Father.

ERNEST
The ball was a good foot out; at the height it was coming when it passed me.

COLONEL [Staring at him.]
You're a—you're aa theorist! From where you were you could n't see the ball at all. [To **LETTY**.] Where's your mother?

LETTY [Emphatically.]
In the blue room, Father!

[The **COLONEL** glares confusedly, and goes away towards the blue room.]

ERNEST [In the swing, and with a smile.]
Your old Dad'll never be a sportsman!

LETTY [Indignantly.]
I wish you wouldn't call Father old, Ernie! What time's Molly coming, Peachey?

[**ROSE** has come from the house, and stands waiting for a chance to speak.

ERNEST [Breaking in.]
Your old Dad's only got one fault: he can't take an impersonal view of things.

MISS BEECH
Can you find me any one who can?

ERNEST [With a smile.]
Well, Peachey!

MISS BEECH [Ironically.]
Oh! of course, there's you!

ERNEST
I don't know about that! But—

ROSE [To **LETTY**.]
Please, Miss, the Missis says will you and Mr. Ernest please to move your things into Miss Peachey's room.

ERNEST [Vexed.]
Deuce of a nuisance havin' to turn out for this fellow Lever. What did Molly want to bring him for?

MISS BEECH
Course you've no personal feeling in the matter!

ROSE [Speaking to **MISS BEECH**.]
The Missis says you're to please move your things into the blue room, please Miss.

LETTY
Aha, Peachey! That settles you! Come on, Ernie!

[She goes towards the house. **ERNEST**, rising from the swing, turns to **MISS BEECH**, who follows.

ERNEST [Smiling, faintly superior.]
Personal, not a bit! I only think while Molly 's out at grass, she oughtn't to—

MISS BEECH [Sharply.]
Oh! do you?

[She hustles **ERNEST** out through the wall, but his voice is heard faintly from the distance: "I think it's jolly thin."

ROSE [To **DICK**.]
The Missis says you're to take all your worms and things, Sir, and put them where they won't be seen.

DICK [Shortly.]
Have n't got any!

ROSE
The Missis says she'll be very angry if you don't put your worms away; and would you come and help kill earwigs in the blue—?

DICK
Hang!

[He goes, and **ROSE** is left alone.]

ROSE [Looking straight before her.]
Please, Miss Joy, the Missis says will you go to her about your frock.

[There is a little pause, then from the hollow tree joy's voice is heard.

JOY
No-o!

ROSE
If you did n't come, I was to tell you she was going to put you in the blue.

[**JOY** looks out of the tree.

[Immovable, but smiling.

Oh, Miss joy, you've done your hair up! [Joy retires into the tree.] Please, Miss, what shall I tell the Missis?

JOY [Joy's voice is heard.]
Anything you like.

ROSE [Over her shoulder.]
I shall be drove to tell her a story, Miss.

JOY
All right! Tell it.

[**ROSE** goes away, and **JOY** comes out. She sits on the rustic seat and waits. **DICK**, coming softly from the house, approaches her.]

DICK [Looking at her intently.]
Joy! I wanted to say something

[**JOY** does not look at him, but twists her fingers.

I shan't see you again you know after to-morrow till I come up for the 'Varsity match.

JOY [Smiling.]

But that's next week.

DICK
Must you go home to-morrow?

[**JOY** nods three times.]

[Coming closer.]

I shall miss you so awfully. You don't know how I—

[**JOY** shakes her head.]

Do look at me!

[**JOY** steals a look.]

Oh! Joy!

[Again **JOY** shakes her head.]

JOY [Suddenly.]
Don't!

DICK [Seizing her hand.]
Oh, Joy! Can't you—

JOY [Drawing the hand away.]
Oh! don't.

DICK [Bending his head.]
It's—it's—so—

JOY [Quietly.]
Don't, Dick!

DICK
But I can't help it! It's too much for me, Joy, I must tell you—

[**MRS GWYN** is seen approaching towards the house.]

JOY [Spinning round.]
It's Mother—oh, Mother!

[She rushes at her.

[**MRS GWYN** is a handsome creature of thirty-six, dressed in a muslin frock. She twists her daughter round, and kisses her.

MRS GWYN

How sweet you look with your hair up, Joy! Who 's this?

[Glancing with a smile at **DICK**.

JOY

Dick Merton—in my letters you know.

[She looks at **DICK** as though she wished him gone.

MRS GWYN

How do you do?

DICK [Shaking hands.]

How d 'you do? I think if you'll excuse me —I'll go in.

[He goes uncertainly.

MRS GWYN

What's the matter with him?

JOY

Oh, nothing! [Hugging her.] Mother! You do look such a duck. Why did you come by the towing-path, was n't it cooking?

MRS GWYN [Avoiding her eyes.]

Mr. Lever wanted to go into Mr. Henty's.

[Her manner is rather artificially composed.

JOY [Dully.]

Oh! Is he-is he really coming here, Mother?

MRS GWYN [Whose voice has hardened just a little.]

If Aunt Nell's got a room for him—of course—why not?

JOY [Digging her chin into her mother's shoulder.]

Why couldn't he choose some day when we'd gone? I wanted you all to myself.

MRS GWYN

You are a quaint child—when I was your age—

JOY [Suddenly looking up.]

Oh! Mother, you must have been a chook!

MRS GWYN

Well, I was about twice as old as you, I know that.

JOY
Had you any—any other offers before you were married, Mother?

MRS GWYN [Smilingly.]
Heaps!

JOY [Reflectively.]
Oh!

MRS GWYN
Why? Have you been having any?

JOY [Glancing at **MRS GWYN**, and then down.]
N-o, of course not!

MRS GWYN
Where are they all? Where's Peachey?

JOY
Fussing about somewhere; don't let's hurry! Oh! you duckie— duckie! Aren't there any letters from Dad?

MRS GWYN [In a harder voice.]
Yes, one or two.

JOY [Hesitating.]
Can't I see?

MRS GWYN
I didn't bring them. [Changing the subject obviously.] Help me to tidy—I'm so hot I don't know what to do.

[She takes out a powder-puff bag, with a tiny looking-glass.

JOY
How lovely it'll be to-morrow-going home!

MRS GWYN [With an uneasy look.]
London's dreadfully stuffy, Joy. You 'll only get knocked up again.

JOY [With consternation.]
Oh! but Mother, I must come.

MRS GWYN (Forcing a smile.)
Oh, well, if you must, you must!

[**JOY** makes a dash at her.]

Don't rumple me again. Here's Uncle Tom.

JOY [Quickly.]
Mother, we're going to dance tonight; promise to dance with me—there are three more girls than men, at least—and don't dance too much with—with—you know—because I'm—[dropping her voice and very still]—jealous.

MRS GWYN [Forcing a laugh.]
You are funny!

JOY [Very quickly.]
I haven't made any engagements because of you.

[The COLONEL approaches through the wall.

MRS GWYN
Well, Uncle Tom?

COLONEL [Genially.]
Why, Molly!

[He kisses her.]

What made you come by the towing-path?

JOY
Because it's so much cooler, of course.

COLONEL
Hallo! What's the matter with you? Phew! you've got your hair up! Go and tell your aunt your mother's on the lawn. Cut along!

[JOY goes, blowing a kiss.

Cracked about you, Molly! Simply cracked! We shall miss her when you take her off to-morrow.

[He places a chair for her.

Sit down, sit down, you must be tired in this heat. I 've sent Bob for your things with the wheelbarrow; what have you got?—only a bag, I suppose.

MRS GWYN [Sitting, with a smile.]
That's all, Uncle Tom, except— my trunk and hat-box.

COLONEL
Phew! And what's-his-name brought a bag, I suppose?

MRS GWYN
They're all together. I hope it's not too much, Uncle Tom.

COLONEL [Dubiously.]
Oh! Bob'll manage! I suppose you see a good deal of—of—Lever. That's his brother in the Guards, isn't it?

MRS GWYN
Yes.

COLONEL
Now what does this chap do?

MRS GWYN
What should he do, Uncle Tom? He's a Director.

COLONEL
Guinea-pig! [Dubiously.] Your bringing him down was a good idea.

[**MRS GWYN**, looking at him sidelong, bites her lips.

I should like to have a look at him. But, I say, you know, Molly— mines, mines! There are a lot of these chaps about, whose business is to cook their own dinners. Your aunt thinks—

MRS GWYN
Oh! Uncle Tom, don't tell me what Aunt Nell thinks!

COLONEL
Well-well! Look here, old girl! It's my experience never to—what I mean is—never to trust too much to a man who has to do with mining. I've always refused to have anything to do with mines. If your husband were in England, of course, I'd say nothing.

MRS GWYN [Very still.]
We'd better keep him out of the question, had n't we?

COLONEL
Of course, if you wish it, my dear.

MRS GWYN
Unfortunately, I do.

COLONEL [Nervously.]
Ah! yes, I know; but look here, Molly, your aunt thinks you're in a very delicate position-in fact, she thinks you see too much of young Lever.

MRS GWYN [Stretching herself like an angry cat.]
Does she? And what do you think?

COLONEL
I? I make a point of not thinking. I only know that here he is, and I don't want you to go burning your fingers, eh?

[**MRS GWYN** sits with a vindictive smile.

A gold mine's a gold mine. I don't mean he deliberately—but they take in women and parsons, and—and all sorts of fools. [Looking down.] And then, you know, I can't tell your feelings, my dear, and I don't want to; but a man about town 'll compromise a woman as soon as he'll look at her, and [softly shaking his head] I don't like that, Molly! It 's not the thing!

[**MRS GWYN** sits unmoved, smiling the same smile, and the **COLONEL** gives her a nervous look.

If—if you were any other woman I should n't care—and if—if you were a plain woman, damme, you might do what you liked! I know you and Geoff don't get on; but here's this child of yours, devoted to you, and—and don't you see, old girl? Eh?

MRS GWYN [With a little hard laugh.]
Thanks! Perfectly! I suppose as you don't think, Uncle Tom, it never occurred to you that I have rather a lonely time of it.

COLONEL [With compunction.]
Oh! my dear, yes, of course I know it must be beastly.

MRS GWYN [Stonily.]
It is.

COLONEL
Yes, yes! [Speaking in a surprised voice.] I don't know what I 'm talking like this for! It's your aunt! She goes on at me till she gets on my nerves. What d' you think she wants me to do now? Put money into this gold mine! Did you ever hear such folly?

MRS GWYN [Breaking into laughter.]
Oh! Uncle Tom!

COLONEL
All very well for you to laugh, Molly!

MRS GWYN [Calmly.]
And how much are you going to put in?

COLONEL
Not a farthing! Why, I've got nothing but my pension and three thousand India stock!

MRS GWYN
Only ninety pounds a year, besides your pension! D' you mean to say that's all you've got, Uncle Tom? I never knew that before. What a shame!

COLONEL [Feelingly.]

It is a d—d shame! I don't suppose there's another case in the army of a man being treated as I've been.

MRS GWYN

But how on earth do you manage here on so little?

COLONEL [Brooding.]

Your aunt's very funny. She's a born manager. She 'd manage the hind leg off a donkey; but if I want five shillings for a charity or what not, I have to whistle for it. And then all of a sudden, Molly, she'll take it into her head to spend goodness knows what on some trumpery or other and come to me for the money. If I have n't got it to give her, out she flies about 3 per cent., and worries me to invest in some wild-cat or other, like your friend's thing, the Jaco what is it? I don't pay the slightest attention to her.

MRS HOPE [From the direction of the house.]

Tom!

COLONEL [Rising.]

Yes, dear! [Then dropping his voice.] I say, Molly, don't you mind what I said about young Lever. I don't want you to imagine that I think harm of people—you know I don't—but so many women come to grief, and—[hotly]—I can't stand men about town; not that he of course—

MRS HOPE [Peremptorily.]

Tom!

COLONEL [In hasty confidence.]

I find it best to let your aunt run on. If she says anything—

MRS HOPE

To-om!

COLONEL

Yes, dear!

[He goes hastily. **MRS GWYN** sits drawing circles on the ground with her charming parasol. Suddenly she springs to her feet, and stands waiting like an animal at bay. The **COLONEL** and **MRS HOPE** approach her talking.

MRS HOPE

Well, how was I to know?

COLONEL

Did n't Joy come and tell you?

MRS HOPE

I don't know what's the matter with that child? Well, Molly, so here you are. You're before your time—that train's always late.

MRS GWYN [With faint irony.]

I'm sorry, Aunt Nell!

[They bob, seem to take fright, and kiss each other gingerly.

MRS HOPE
What have you done with Mr. Lever? I shall have to put him in Peachey's room. Tom's got no champagne.

COLONEL
They've a very decent brand down at the George, Molly, I'll send Bob over—

MRS HOPE
Rubbish, Tom! He'll just have to put up with what he can get!

MRS GWYN
Of course! He's not a snob! For goodness sake, Aunt Nell, don't put yourself out! I'm sorry I suggested his coming.

COLONEL
My dear, we ought to have champagne in the house—in case of accident.

MRS GWYN [Shaking him gently by the coat.] No, please, Uncle Tom!

MRS HOPE [Suddenly.]
Now, I've told your uncle, Molly, that he's not to go in for this gold mine without making certain it's a good thing. Mind, I think you've been very rash. I'm going to give you a good talking to; and that's not all—you ought n't to go about like this with a young man; he's not at all bad looking. I remember him perfectly well at the Fleming's dance.

[On **MRS GWYN'S** lips there comes a little mocking smile.

COLONEL [Pulling his wife's sleeve.]
Nell!

MRS HOPE
No, Tom, I'm going to talk to Molly; she's old enough to know better.

MRS GWYN
Yes?

MRS HOPE
Yes, and you'll get yourself into a mess; I don't approve of it, and when I see a thing I don't approve of—

COLONEL [Walking about, and pulling his moustache.]
Nell, I won't have it, I simply won't have it.

MRS HOPE
What rate of interest are these Preference shares to pay?

MRS GWYN [Still smiling.]
Ten per cent.

MRS HOPE
What did I tell you, Tom? And are they safe?

MRS GWYN
You'd better ask Maurice.

MRS HOPE
There, you see, you call him Maurice! Now supposing your uncle went in for some of them—

COLONEL [Taking off his hat-in a high, hot voice]
I'm not going in for anything of the sort.

MRS HOPE
Don't swing your hat by the brim! Go and look if you can see him coming!

[The **COLONEL** goes.]

[In a lower voice.] Your uncle's getting very bald. I 've only shoulder of lamb for lunch, and a salad. It's lucky it's too hot to eat.

[**MISS BEECH** has appeared while she is speaking.

Here she is, Peachey!

MISS BEECH
I see her.

[She kisses **MRS GWYN**, and looks at her intently.

MRS GWYN [Shrugging her shoulders.]
Well, Peachey! What d 'you make of me?

COLONEL [Returning from his search.]
There's a white hat crossing the second stile. Is that your friend, Molly?

[**MRS GWYN** nods.]

MRS HOPE
Oh! before I forget, Peachey—Letty and Ernest can move their things back again. I'm going to put Mr. Lever in your room.

[Catching sight of the paint pot on the ground.]

There's that disgusting paint pot! Take it up at once, Tom, and put it in the tree.

[The **COLONEL** picks up the pot and bears it to the hollow tree followed by **MRS HOPE**; he enters.

MRS HOPE [Speaking into the tree.]
Not there!

COLONEL [From within.]
Well, where then?

MRS HOPE
Why—up—oh! gracious!

[**MRS GWYN**, standing alone, is smiling. **LEVER** approaches from the towing-path. He is a man like a fencer's wrist, supple and steely. A man whose age is difficult to tell, with a quick, good-looking face, and a line between his brows; his darkish hair is flecked with grey. He gives the feeling that he has always had to spurt to keep pace with his own life.

MRS HOPE [Also entering the hollow tree.]
No-oh!

COLONEL [From the depths, in a high voice.]
Well, dash it then! What do you want?

MRS GWYN
Peachey, may I introduce Mr. Lever to you? Miss Beech, my old governess.

[They shake each other by the hand.

LEVER
How do you do?

[His voice is pleasant, his manner easy.

MISS BEECH
Pleased to meet you.

[Her manner is that of one who is not pleased. She watches.

MRS GWYN [Pointing to the tree-maliciously.]
This is my uncle and my aunt. They're taking exercise, I think.

[The **COLONEL** and **MRS HOPE** emerge convulsively. They are very hot. **LEVER** and **MRS. GWYN** are very cool.

MRS HOPE [Shaking hands with him.]
So you 've got here! Are n't you very hot?—Tom!

COLONEL

Brought a splendid day with you! Splendid!

[As he speaks, Joy comes running with a bunch of roses; seeing **LEVER**, she stops and stands quite rigid.]

MISS BEECH [Sitting in the swing.]
Thunder!

COLONEL
Thunder? Nonsense, Peachey, you're always imagining something. Look at the sky!

MISS BEECH
Thunder!

[**MRS GWYN's** smile has faded.]

MRS HOPE [Turning.]
Joy, don't you see Mr. Lever?

[**JOY**, turning to her mother, gives her the roses. With a forced smile, **LEVER** advances, holding out his hand.

LEVER
How are you, Joy? Have n't seen you for an age!

JOY [Without expression.]
I am very well, thank you.

[She raises her hand, and just touches his. **MRS GWYN'S** eyes are fixed on her daughter. **MISS BEECH** is watching them intently. **MRS HOPE** is buttoning the **COLONEL'S** coat.

ACT II

It is afternoon, and at a garden-table placed beneath the hollow tree, the **COLONEL** is poring over plans. Astride of a garden-chair, **LEVER** is smoking cigarettes. **DICK** is hanging Chinese lanterns to the hollow tree.

LEVER
Of course, if this level [pointing with his cigarette] peters out to the West we shall be in a tightish place; you know what a mine is at this stage, Colonel Hope.

COLONEL [Absently.]
Yes, yes. [Tracing a line.] What is there to prevent its running out here to the East?

LEVER
Well, nothing, except that as a matter of fact it doesn't.

COLONEL [With some excitement.]

I'm very glad you showed me these papers, very glad! I say that it's a most astonishing thing if the ore suddenly stops there. [A gleam of humour visits **LEVER'S** face.] I'm not an expert, but you ought to prove that ground to the East more thoroughly.

LEVER [Quizzically.]

Of course, sir, if you advise that—

COLONEL

If it were mine, I'd no more sit down under the belief that the ore stopped there than I 'd—There's a harmony in these things.

LEVER

I can only tell you what our experts say.

COLONEL

Ah! Experts! No faith in them—never had! Miners, lawyers, theologians, cowardly lot—pays them to be cowardly. When they have n't their own axes to grind, they've got their theories; a theory's a dangerous thing.

[He loses himself in contemplation of the papers.

Now my theory is, you 're in strata here of what we call the Triassic Age.

LEVER [Smiling faintly.]

Ah!

COLONEL

You've struck a fault, that's what's happened. The ore may be as much as thirty or forty yards out; but it 's there, depend on it.

LEVER

Would you back that opinion, sir?

COLONEL [With dignity.]

I never give an opinion that I'm not prepared to back. I want to get to the bottom of this. What's to prevent the gold going down indefinitely?

LEVER

Nothing, so far as I know.

COLONEL [With suspicion.]

Eh!

LEVER

All I can tell you is: This is as far as we've got, and we want more money before we can get any farther.

COLONEL [Absently.]

Yes, yes; that's very usual.

LEVER
If you ask my personal opinion I think it's very doubtful that the gold does go down.

COLONEL [Smiling.]
Oh! a personal opinion a matter of this sort!

LEVER [As though about to take the papers.]
Perhaps we'd better close the sitting, sir; sorry to have bored you.

COLONEL
Now, now! Don't be so touchy! If I'm to put money in, I'm bound to look at it all round.

LEVER [With lifted brows.]
Please don't imagine that I want you to put money in.

COLONEL
Confound it, sir! D 'you suppose I take you for a Company promoter?

LEVER
Thank you!

COLONEL [Looking at him doubtfully.]
You've got Irish blood in you—um? You're so hasty!

LEVER
If you 're really thinking of taking shares—my advice to you is, don't!

COLONEL [Regretfully.]
If this were an ordinary gold mine, I wouldn't dream of looking at it, I want you to understand that. Nobody has a greater objection to gold mines than I.

LEVER [Looks down at his host with half-closed eyes.]
But it is a gold mine, Colonel Hope.

COLONEL
I know, I know; but I 've been into it for myself; I've formed my opinion personally. Now, what 's the reason you don't want me to invest?

LEVER
Well, if it doesn't turn out as you expect, you'll say it's my doing. I know what investors are.

COLONEL [Dubiously.]
If it were a Westralian or a Kaffir I would n't touch it with a pair of tongs! It 's not as if I were going to put much in!

[He suddenly bends above the papers as though magnetically attracted.

I like these Triassic formations!

[**DICK**, who has hung the last lantern, moodily departs.]

LEVER [Looking after him.]
That young man seems depressed.

COLONEL [As though remembering his principles.]
I don't like mines, never have! [Suddenly absorbed again.] I tell you what, Lever—this thing's got tremendous possibilities. You don't seem to believe in it enough. No mine's any good without faith; until I see for myself, however, I shan't commit myself beyond a thousand.

LEVER
Are you serious, sir?

COLONEL
Certainly! I've been thinking it over ever since you told me Henty had fought shy. I 've a poor opinion of Henty. He's one of those fellows that says one thing and does another. An opportunist!

LEVER [Slowly.]
I'm afraid we're all that, more or less.

[He sits beneath the hollow tree.

COLONEL
A man never knows what he is himself. There 's my wife. She thinks she 's—By the way, don't say anything to her about this, please. And, Lever [nervously], I don't think, you know, this is quite the sort of thing for my niece.

LEVER [Quietly.]
I agree. I mean to get her out of it.

COLONEL [A little taken aback.]
Ah! You know, she—she's in a very delicate position, living by herself in London. [**LEVER** looks at him ironically.] You [very nervously] see a good deal of her? If it had n't been for Joy growing so fast, we shouldn't have had the child down here. Her mother ought to have her with her. Eh! Don't you think so?

LEVER [Forcing a smile.]
Mrs. Gwyn always seems to me to get on all right.

COLONEL [As though making a discovery.]
You know, I've found that when a woman's living alone and unprotected, the very least thing will set a lot of hags and jackanapes talking. [Hotly.] The more unprotected and helpless a woman is, the more they revel in it. If there's anything I hate in this world, it's those wretched creatures who babble about their neighbours' affairs.

LEVER
I agree with you.

COLONEL
One ought to be very careful not to give them—that is— [checks himself confused; then hurrying on]—I suppose you and Joy get on all right?

LEVER [Coolly.]
Pretty well, thanks. I'm not exactly in Joy's line; have n't seen very much of her, in fact.

[**MISS BEECH** and **JOY** have been approaching from the house. But seeing **LEVER**, **JOY** turns abruptly, hesitates a moment, and with an angry gesture goes away.

COLONEL [Unconscious.]
Wonderfully affectionate little thing! Well, she'll be going home to-morrow!

MISS BEECH [Who has been gazing after **JOY**.]
Talkin' business, poor creatures?

LEVER
Oh, no! If you'll excuse me, I'll wash my hands before tea.

[He glances at the **COLONEL** poring over papers, and, shrugging his shoulders, strolls away.

MISS BEECH [Sitting in the swing.]
I see your horrid papers.

COLONEL
Be quiet, Peachey!

MISS BEECH
On a beautiful summer's day, too.

COLONEL
That'll do now.

MISS BEECH [Unmoved.]
For every ounce you take out of a gold mine you put two in.

COLONEL
Who told you that rubbish?

MISS BEECH [With devilry.]
You did!

COLONEL
This is n't an ordinary gold mine.

MISS BEECH
Oh! quite a special thing.

[**COLONEL** stares at her, but subsiding at hey impassivity, he pores again over the papers.

[**ROSE** has approached with a tea cloth.]

ROSE
If you please, sir, the Missis told me to lay the tea.

COLONEL
Go away! Ten fives fifty. Ten 5 16ths, Peachey?

MISS BEECH
I hate your nasty sums!

[**ROSE** goes away. The **COLONEL** Writes. **MRS HOPE'S** voice is heard, "Now then, bring those chairs, you two. Not that one, Ernest." **ERNEST** and **LETTY** appear through the openings of the wall, each with a chair.]

COLONEL [With dull exasperation.]
What do you want?

LETTY
Tea, Father.

[She places her chair and goes away.

ERNEST
That Johnny-bird Lever is too cocksure for me, Colonel. Those South American things are no good at all. I know all about them from young Scrotton. There's not one that's worth a red cent. If you want a flutter—

COLONEL [Explosively.]
Flutter! I'm not a gambler, sir!

ERNEST
Well, Colonel [with a smile], I only don't want you to chuck your money away on a stiff 'un. If you want anything good you should go to Mexico.

COLONEL [Jumping up and holding out the map.]
Go to [He stops in time.] What d'you call that, eh? M-E-X—

ERNEST [Not to be embarrassed.]
It all depend on what part.

COLONEL

You think you know everything—you think nothing's right unless it's your own idea! Be good enough to keep your advice to yourself.

ERNEST [Moving with his chair, and stopping with a smile.]
If you ask me, I should say it wasn't playing the game to put Molly into a thing like that.

COLONEL
What do you mean, sir?

ERNEST
Any Juggins can see that she's a bit gone on our friend.

COLONEL [Freezingly.]
Indeed!

ERNEST
He's not at all the sort of Johnny that appeals to me.

COLONEL
Really?

ERNEST [Unmoved.]
If I were you, Colonel, I should tip her the wink. He was hanging about her at Ascot all the time. It's a bit thick!

[**MRS HOPE** followed by **ROSE** appears from the house.

COLONEL [Stammering with passion.]
Jackanapes!

MRS HOPE
Don't stand there, Tom; clear those papers, and let Rose lay the table. Now, Ernest, go and get another chair.

[The **COLONEL** looks wildly round and sits beneath the hollow tree, with his head held in his hands. **ROSE** lays the cloth.

MRS BEECH [Sitting beside the **COLONEL**.]
Poor creature!

ERNEST [Carrying his chair about with him.]
Ask any Johnny in the City, he'll tell you Mexico's a very tricky country—the people are awful rotters—

MRS HOPE
Put that chair down, Ernest.

[**ERNEST** looks at the chair, puts it down, opens his mouth, and goes away. **ROSE** follows him.

What's he been talking about? You oughtn't to get so excited, Tom; is your head bad, old man? Here, take these papers!

[She hands the papers to the **COLONEL**.

Peachey, go in and tell them tea 'll be ready in a minute, there 's a good soul? Oh! and on my dressing table you'll find a bottle of Eau de Cologne.

MRS. BEECH
Don't let him get in a temper again. That 's three times to-day!

[She goes towards the house.

COLONEL
Never met such a fellow in my life, the most opinionated, narrow-minded—thinks he knows everything. Whatever Letty could see in him I can't think. Pragmatical beggar!

MRS HOPE
Now Tom! What have you been up to, to get into a state like this?

COLONEL [Avoiding her eyes.]
I shall lose my temper with him one of these days. He's got that confounded habit of thinking nobody can be right but himself.

MRS HOPE
That's enough! I want to talk to you seriously! Dick's in love. I'm perfectly certain of it.

COLONEL
Love! Who's he in love with—Peachey?

MRS HOPE
You can see it all over him. If I saw any signs of Joy's breaking out, I'd send them both away. I simply won't have it.

COLONEL
Why, she's a child!

MRS HOPE [Pursuing her own thoughts.]
But she isn't—not yet. I've been watching her very carefully. She's more in love with her Mother than any one, follows her about like a dog! She's been quite rude to Mr. Lever.

COLONEL [Pursuing his own thoughts.]
I don't believe a word of it.

[He rises and walks about]

MRS HOPE
Don't believe a word of what?

[The **COLONEL** is Silent.

[Pursuing his thoughts with her own.

If I thought there was anything between Molly and Mr. Lever, d 'you suppose I'd have him in the house?

[The **COLONEL** stops, and gives a sort of grunt.

He's a very nice fellow; and I want you to pump him well, Tom, and see what there is in this mine.

COLONEL [Uneasily.]
Pump!

MRS HOPE [Looking at him curiously.]
Yes, you 've been up to something! Now what is it?

COLONEL
Pump my own guest! I never heard of such a thing!

MRS HOPE
There you are on your high horse! I do wish you had a little common-sense, Tom!

COLONEL
I'd as soon you asked me to sneak about eavesdropping! Pump!

MRS HOPE
Well, what were you looking at these papers for? It does drive me so wild the way you throw away all the chances you have of making a little money. I've got you this opportunity, and you do nothing but rave up and down, and talk nonsense!

COLONEL [In a high voice]
Much you know about it! I 've taken a thousand shares in this mine—

[He stops dead. There is a silence.]

MRS HOPE
You 've—WHAT? Without consulting me? Well, then, you 'll just go and take them out again!

COLONEL
You want me to—?

MRS HOPE
The idea! As if you could trust your judgment in a thing like that! You 'll just go at once and say there was a mistake; then we 'll talk it over calmly.

COLONEL [Drawing himself up.]

Go back on what I 've said? Not if I lose every penny! First you worry me to take the shares, and then you worry me not—I won't have it, Nell, I won't have it!

MRS HOPE
Well, if I'd thought you'd have forgotten what you said this morning and turned about like this, d'you suppose I'd have spoken to you at all? Now, do you?

COLONEL
Rubbish! If you can't see that this is a special opportunity!

[He walks away followed by **MRS HOPE**, who endeavors to make him see her point of view. **ERNEST** and **LETTY** are now returning from the house armed with a third chair.

LETTY
What's the matter with everybody? Is it the heat?

ERNEST [Preoccupied and sitting in the swing.]
That sportsman, Lever, you know, ought to be warned off.

LETTY [Signing to **ERNEST**.]
Where's Miss Joy, Rose?

ROSE
Don't know, Miss.

[Putting down the tray, she goes.

[**ROSE**, has followed with the tea tray.]

LETTY
Ernie, be careful, you never know where Joy is.

ERNEST [Preoccupied with his reflections.]
Your old Dad 's as mad as a hatter with me.

LETTY
Why?

ERNEST
Well, I merely said what I thought, that Molly ought to look out what's she's doing, and he dropped on me like a cartload of bricks.

LETTY
The Dad's very fond of Molly.

ERNEST
But look here, d'you mean to tell me that she and Lever are n't—

LETTY

Don't! Suppose they are! If joy were to hear it'd be simply awful. I like Molly. I 'm not going to believe anything against her. I don't see the use of it. If it is, it is, and if it is n't, it is n't.

ERNEST

Well, all I know is that when I told her the mine was probably a frost she went for me like steam.

LETTY

Well, so should I. She was only sticking up for her friends.

ERNEST

Ask the old Peachey-bird. She knows a thing or two. Look here, I don't mind a man's being a bit of a sportsman, but I think Molly's bringin' him down here is too thick. Your old Dad's got one of his notions that because this Josser's his guest, he must keep him in a glass case, and take shares in his mine, and all the rest of it.

LETTY

I do think people are horrible, always thinking things. It's not as if Molly were a stranger. She's my own cousin. I 'm not going to believe anything about my own cousin. I simply won't.

ERNEST [Reluctantly realising the difference that this makes.]
I suppose it does make a difference, her bein' your cousin.

LETTY

Of course it does! I only hope to goodness no one will make Joy suspect—

[She stops and buts her finger to her lips, for **JOY** is coming towards them, as the tea-bell sounds. She is followed by **DICK** and **MISS BEECH** with the Eau de Cologne. The **COLONEL** and **MRS HOPE** are also coming back, discussing still each other's point of view.

JOY

Where 's Mother? Isn't she here?

MRS HOPE

Now Joy, come and sit down; your mother's been told tea's ready; if she lets it get cold it's her lookout.

DICK [Producing a rug, and spreading it beneath the tree.]
Plenty of room, Joy.

JOY

I don't believe Mother knows, Aunt Nell.

[**MRS GWYN** and **LEVER** appear in the opening of the wall.]

LETTY [Touching **ERNEST's** arm.]
Look, Ernie! Four couples and Peachey—

ERNEST [Preoccupied.]

What couples?

JOY
Oh! Mums, here you are!

[Seizing her, she turns her back on **LEVER.** They sit in various seats, and **MRS HOPE** pours out the tea.

MRS HOPE
Hand the sandwiches to Mr. Lever, Peachey. It's our own jam, Mr. Lever.

LEVER
Thanks.

[He takes a bite.

It's splendid!

MRS GWYN [With forced gaiety.]
It's the first time I've ever seen you eat jam.

LEVER [Smiling a forced smile.]
Really! But I love it.

MRS GWYN [With a little bow.]
You always refuse mine.

JOY [Who has been staring at her enemy, suddenly.]
I'm all burnt up! Are n't you simply boiled, Mother?

[She touches her Mother's forehead.

MRS GWYN
Ugh! You're quite clammy, Joy.

JOY
It's enough to make any one clammy.

[Her eyes go back to **LEVER'S** face as though to stab him.

ERNEST [From the swing.]
I say, you know, the glass is going down.

LEVER [Suavely.]
The glass in the hall's steady enough.

ERNEST
Oh, I never go by that; that's a rotten old glass.

COLONEL
Oh! is it?

ERNEST [Paying no attention.]
I've got a little ripper—never puts you in the cart. Bet you what you like we have thunder before tomorrow night.

MISS BEECH [Removing her gaze from **JOY** to **LEVER**.]
You don't think we shall have it before to-night, do you?

LEVER [Suavely.]
I beg your pardon; did you speak to me?

MISS BEECH
I said, you don't think we shall have the thunder before to-night, do you?

[She resumes her watch on joy.

LEVER [Blandly.]
Really, I don't see any signs of it.

[**JOY**, crossing to the rug, flings herself down. And **DICK** sits cross-legged, with his eyes fast fixed on her.

MISS BEECH [Eating.]
People don't often see what they don't want to, do they?

[**LEVER** only lifts his brows.]

MRS GWYN [Quickly breaking ivy.]
What are you talking about? The weather's perfect.

MISS BEECH
Isn't it?

MRS HOPE
You'd better make a good tea, Peachey; nobody'll get anything till eight, and then only cold shoulder. You must just put up with no hot dinner, Mr. Lever.

LEVER [Bowing.]
Whatever is good enough for Miss Beech is good enough for me.

MISS BEECH [Sardonically-taking another sandwich.]
So you think!

MRS GWYN [With forced gaiety.]
Don't be so absurd, Peachey.

[**MISS BEECH**, grunts slightly.]

COLONEL [Once more busy with his papers.]
I see the name of your engineer is Rodriguez—Italian, eh?

LEVER
Portuguese.

COLONEL
Don't like that!

LEVER
I believe he was born in England.

COLONEL [Reassured.]
Oh, was he? Ah!

ERNEST
Awful rotters, those Portuguese!

COLONEL
There you go!

LETTY
Well, Father, Ernie only said what you said.

MRS HOPE
Now I want to ask you, Mr. Lever, is this gold mine safe? If it isn't—I simply won't allow Tom to take these shares; he can't afford it.

LEVER
It rather depends on what you call safe, Mrs. Hope.

MRS HOPE
I don't want anything extravagant, of course; if they're going to pay their 10 per cent, regularly, and Tom can have his money out at any time—

[There is a faint whistle from the swing.

I only want to know that it's a thoroughly genuine thing.

MRS GWYN [Indignantly.]
As if Maurice would be a Director if it was n't?

MRS HOPE
Now Molly, I'm simply asking—

MRS GWYN
Yes, you are!

COLONEL [Rising.]
I'll take two thousand of those shares, Lever. To have my wife talk like that—I 'm quite ashamed.

LEVER
Oh, come, sir, Mrs. Hope only meant—

[**MRS GWYN** looks eagerly at **LEVER**.

DICK [Quietly.]
Let's go on the river, Joy.

[**JOY** rises, and goes to her Mother's chair.]

MRS HOPE
Of course! What rubbish, Tom! As if any one ever invested money without making sure!

LEVER [Ironically.]
It seems a little difficult to make sure in this case. There isn't the smallest necessity for Colonel Hope to take any shares, and it looks to me as if he'd better not.

[He lights a cigarette.

MRS HOPE
Now, Mr. Lever, don't be offended! I'm very anxious for Tom to take the shares if you say the thing's so good.

LEVER
I 'm afraid I must ask to be left out, please.

JOY [Whispering.]
Mother, if you've finished, do come, I want to show you my room.

MRS HOPE
I would n't say a word, only Tom's so easily taken in.

MRS GWYN [Fiercely.]
Aunt Nell, how can't you?

[**JOY** gives a little savage laugh.

LETTY [Hastily.]
Ernie, will you play Dick and me? Come on, Dick!

[All three go out towards the lawn.

MRS HOPE

You ought to know your Uncle by this time, Molly. He's just like a child. He'd be a pauper to-morrow if I did n't see to things.

COLONEL
Understand once for all that I shall take two thousand shares in this mine. I 'm—I 'm humiliated.

[He turns and goes towards the house.

MRS HOPE
Well, what on earth have I said?

[She hurries after him.

MRS GWYN [In a low voice as she passes.]
You need n't insult my friends!

[**LEVER**, shrugging his shoulders, has strolled aside. **JOY**, with a passionate movement seen only by **MISS BEECH**, goes off towards the house. **MISS BEECH** and **MRS GWYN** aye left alone beside the remnants of the feast.

MISS BEECH
Molly!

[**MRS GWYN** looks up startled.]

Take care, Molly, take care! The child! Can't you see? [Apostrophising **LEVER**.] Take care, Molly, take care!

LEVER [Coming back.]
Awfully hot, is n't it?

MISS BEECH
Ah! and it'll be hotter if we don't mind.

LEVER
[Suavely.] Do we control these things?

[**MISS BEECH** looking from face to face, nods her head repeatedly; then gathering her skirts she walks towards the house. **MRS GWYN** sits motionless, staying before her.

Extraordinary old lady!

[He pitches away his cigarette.

What's the matter with her, Molly?

MRS GWYN [With an effort.]
Oh! Peachey's a character!

LEVER [Frowning.]
So I see!

[There is a silence.

MRS GWYN
Maurice!

LEVER
Yes.

MRS GWYN
Aunt Nell's hopeless, you mustn't mind her.

LEVER [In a dubious and ironic voice.]
My dear girl, I 've too much to bother me to mind trifles like that.

MRS GWYN [Going to him suddenly.]
Tell me, won't you?

[**LEVER** shrugs his shoulders.]
A month ago you'd have told me soon enough!

LEVER
Now, Molly!

MRS GWYN
Ah! [With a bitter smile.] The Spring's soon over.

LEVER
It 's always Spring between us.

MRS GWYN
Is it?

LEVER
You did n't tell me what you were thinking about just now when you sat there like stone.

MRS GWYN
It does n't do for a woman to say too much.

LEVER
Have I been so bad to you that you need feel like that, Molly?

MRS GWYN [With a little warm squeeze of his arm.]
Oh! my dear, it's only that I'm so—

[She stops.]

LEVER [Gently].
So what?

MRS GWYN [In a low voice.]
It's hateful here.

LEVER
I didn't want to come. I don't understand why you suggested it.

[**MRS GWYN** is silent.]

It's been a mistake.

MRS GWYN [Her eyes fixed on the ground.]
Joy comes home to-morrow. I thought if I brought you here—I should know—

LEVER [Vexedly.]
Um!

MRS GWYN [Losing her control.]
Can't you SEE? It haunts me? How are we to go on? I must know—I must know!

LEVER
I don't see that my coming—

MRS GWYN
I thought I should have more confidence; I thought I should be able to face it better in London, if you came down here openly—and now—I feel I must n't speak or look at you.

LEVER
You don't think your Aunt—

MRS GWYN [Scornfully.]
She! It's only Joy I care about.

LEVER [Frowning.]
We must be more careful, that's all. We mustn't give ourselves away again, as we were doing just now.

MRS GWYN
When any one says anything horrid to you, I can't help it.

[She puts her hand on the label of his coat.

LEVER
My dear child, take care!

[**MRS GWYN** drops her hand. She throws her head back, and her throat is seen to work as though she were gulping down a bitter draught. She moves away.

LEVER [Following hastily.]
Don't dear, don't! I only meant—Come, Molly, let's be sensible. I want to tell you something about the mine.

MRS GWYN [With a quavering smile.]
Yes-let 's talk sensibly, and walk properly in this sensible, proper place.

[**LEVER** is seen trying to soothe her, and yet to walk properly. As they disappear, they are viewed by **JOY**, who, like the shadow parted from its figure, has come to join it again. She stands now, foiled, a carnation in her hand; then flings herself on a chair, and leans her elbows on the table.]

JOY
I hate him! Pig!

ROSE [Who has come to clear the tea things.]
Did you call, Miss?

JOY
Not you!

ROSE [Motionless.]
No, Miss!

JOY [Leaning back and tearing the flower.]
Oh! do hurry up, Rose!

ROSE [Collects the tea things.]
Mr. Dick's coming down the path! Aren't I going to get you to do your frock, Miss Joy?

JOY
No.

ROSE
What will the Missis say?

JOY
Oh, don't be so stuck, Rose!

[**ROSE** goes, but **DICK** has come.]

DICK
Come on the river, Joy, just for half an hour, as far as the kingfishers—do!

[**JOY** shakes her head.

Why not? It'll be so jolly and cool. I'm most awfully sorry if I worried you this morning. I didn't mean to. I won't again, I promise.

[JOY slides a look at him, and from that look he gains a little courage.

Do come! It'll be the last time. I feel it awfully, Joy.

JOY
There's nothing to hurt you!

DICK [Gloomily.]
Isn't there—when you're like this?

JOY [In a hard voice.]
If you don't like me, why do you follow me about?

DICK
What is the matter?

JOY [Looking up, as if for want of air.]
Oh! Don't!

DICK
Oh, Joy, what is the matter? Is it the heat?

JOY [With a little laugh.]
Yes.

DICK
Have some Eau de Cologne. I'll make you a bandage.

[He takes the Eau de Cologne, and makes a bandage with his handkerchief.

It's quite clean.

JOY
Oh, Dick, you are so funny!

DICK [Bandaging her forehead.]
I can't bear you to feel bad; it puts me off completely. I mean I don't generally make a fuss about people, but when it's you—

JOY [Suddenly.]
I'm all right.

DICK
Is that comfy?

JOY [With her chin up, and her eyes fast closed.]
Quite.

DICK
I'm not going to stay and worry you. You ought to rest. Only, Joy! Look here! If you want me to do anything for you, any time—

JOY [Half opening her eyes.]
Only to go away.

[**DICK** bites his lips and walks away.]

Dick—[softly]—Dick!

[**DICK** stops.

I didn't mean that; will you get me some water-irises for this evening?

DICK
Won't I? [He goes to the hollow tree and from its darkness takes a bucket and a boat-hook.] I know where there are some rippers!

[**JOY** stays unmoving with her eyes half closed.

Are you sure you 're all right. Joy? You 'll just rest here in the shade, won't you, till I come back?—it 'll do you no end of good. I shan't be twenty minutes.

[He goes, but cannot help returning softly, to make sure.

You're quite sure you 're all right?

[**JOY** nods. He goes away towards the river. But there is no rest for **JOY.** The voices of **MRS GWYN** and **LEVER** are heard returning.

JOY [With a gesture of anger.]
Hateful! Hateful!

[She runs away.]

[**MRS GWYN** and **LEVER** are seen approaching; they pass the tree, in conversation.

MRS GWYN
But I don't see why, Maurice.

LEVER
We mean to sell the mine; we must do some more work on it, and for that we must have money.

MRS GWYN

If you only want a little, I should have thought you could have got it in a minute in the City.

LEVER [Shaking his head.]
No, no; we must get it privately.

MRS GWYN [Doubtfully.]
Oh! [She slowly adds.] Then it isn't such a good thing!

[And she does not look at him.]

LEVER
Well, we mean to sell it.

MRS GWYN
What about the people who buy?

LEVER [Dubiously regarding her.]
My dear girl, they've just as much chance as we had. It 's not my business to think of them. There's YOUR thousand pounds—

MRS GWYN [Softly.]
Don't bother about my money, Maurice. I don't want you to do anything not quite—

LEVER [Evasively.]
Oh! There's my brother's and my sister's too. I 'm not going to let any of you run any risk. When we all went in for it the thing looked splendid; it 's only the last month that we 've had doubts. What bothers me now is your Uncle. I don't want him to take these shares. It looks as if I'd come here on purpose.

MRS GWYN
Oh! he mustn't take them!

LEVER
That 's all very well; but it 's not so simple.

MRS GWYN [Shyly.]
But, Maurice, have you told him about the selling?

LEVER [Gloomily, under the hollow tree.]
It 's a Board secret. I'd no business to tell even you.

MRS GWYN
But he thinks he's taking shares in a good—a permanent thing.

LEVER
You can't go into a mining venture without some risk.

MRS GWYN
Oh yes, I know—but—but Uncle Tom is such a dear!

LEVER [Stubbornly.]

I can't help his being the sort of man he is. I did n't want him to take these shares; I told him so in so many words. Put yourself in my place, Molly: how can I go to him and say, "This thing may turn out rotten," when he knows I got you to put your money into it?

[But **JOY**, the lost shadow, has come back. She moves forward resolutely. They are divided from her by the hollow tree; she is unseen. She stops.

MRS GWYN

I think he ought to be told about the selling; it 's not fair.

LEVER

What on earth made him rush at the thing like that? I don't understand that kind of man.

MRS GWYN [Impulsively.]

I must tell him, Maurice; I can't let him take the shares without—

[She puts her hand on his arm.]

[**JOY** turns, as if to go back whence she came, but stops once more.

LEVER [Slowly and very quietly.]

I did n't think you'd give me away, Molly.

MRS GWYN

I don't think I quite understand.

LEVER

If you tell the Colonel about this sale the poor old chap will think me a man that you ought to have nothing to do with. Do you want that?

[**MRS GWYN**, giving her lover a long look, touches his sleeve. **JOY**, slipping behind the hollow tree, has gone.]

You can't act in a case like this as if you 'd only a principle to consider. It 's the—the special circumstances.

MRS GWYN [With a faint smile.]

But you'll be glad to get the money won't you?

LEVER

By George! if you're going to take it like this, Molly

MRS GWYN

Don't!

LEVER

We may not sell after all, dear, we may find it turn out trumps.

MRS GWYN [With a shiver.]
I don't want to hear any more. I know women don't understand. [Impulsively.] It's only that I can't bear any one should think that you—

LEVER [Distressed.]
For goodness sake don't look like that, Molly! Of course, I'll speak to your Uncle. I'll stop him somehow, even if I have to make a fool of myself. I 'll do anything you want—

MRS GWYN
I feel as if I were being smothered here.

LEVER
It 's only for one day.

MRS GWYN [With sudden tenderness.]
It's not your fault, dear. I ought to have known how it would be. Well, let's go in!

[She sets her lips, and walks towards the house with **LEVER** following. But no sooner has she disappeared than **JOY** comes running after; she stops, as though throwing down a challenge. Her cheeks and ears are burning.

JOY
Mother!

[After a moment **MRS GWYN** reappears in the opening of the wall.

MRS GWYN
Oh! here you are!

JOY [Breathlessly.]
Yes.

MRS GWYN [Uncertainly.]
Where—have you been? You look dreadfully hot; have you been running?

JOY
Yes—no.

MRS GWYN [Looking at her fixedly.]
What's the matter—you 're trembling! [Softly.] Are n't you well, dear?

JOY
Yes—I don't know.

MRS GWYN
What is it, darling?

JOY [Suddenly clinging to her.]
Oh! Mother!

MRS GWYN
I don't understand.

JOY [Breathlessly.]
Oh, Mother, let me go back home with you now at once— Mrs Gwyn [Her face hardening.] Why? What on earth—

JOY
I can't stay here.

MRS GWYN
But why?

JOY
I want to be with you—Oh! Mother, don't you love me?

MRS GWYN [With a faint smile.]
Of course I love you, Joy.

JOY
Ah! but you love him more.

MRS GWYN
Love him—whom?

JOY
Oh! Mother, I did n't—

[She tries to take her Mother's hand, but fails.

Oh! don't.

MRS GWYN
You'd better explain what you mean, I think.

JOY
I want to get you to—he—he 's—he 'snot—!

MRS GWYN [Frigidly.]
Really, Joy!

JOY [Passionately.]
I'll fight against him, and I know there's something wrong about—

[She stops.

MRS GWYN
About what?

JOY
Let's tell Uncle Tom, Mother, and go away.

MRS GWYN
Tell Uncle—Tom—what?

JOY [Looking down and almost whispering.]
About—about—the mine.

MRS GWYN
What about the mine? What do you mean? [Fiercely.] Have you been spying on me?

JOY [Shrinking.]
No! oh, no!

MRS GWYN
Where were you?

JOY [Just above her breath.]
I—I heard something.

MRS GWYN [Bitterly.]
But you were not spying?

JOY
I was n't—I wasn't! I didn't want—to hear. I only heard a little. I couldn't help listening, Mother.

MRS GWYN [With a little laugh.]
Couldn't help listening?

JOY [Through her teeth.]
I hate him. I didn't mean to listen, but I hate him.

MRS GWYN
I see. Why do you hate him?

[There is a silence.]

JOY
He—he—[She stops.]

MRS GWYN
Yes?

JOY [With a sort of despair.]
I don't know. Oh! I don't know! But I feel—

MRS GWYN
I can't reason with you. As to what you heard, it 's— ridiculous.

JOY
It 's not that. It 's—it 's you!

MRS GWYN [Stonily.]
I don't know what you mean.

JOY [Passionately.]
I wish Dad were here!

MRS GWYN
Do you love your Father as much as me?

JOY
Oh! Mother, no-you know I don't.

MRS GWYN [Resentfully.]
Then why do you want him?

JOY [Almost under her breath.]
Because of that man.

MRS GWYN
Indeed!

JOY
I will never—never make friends with him.

MRS GWYN [Cuttingly.]
I have not asked you to.

JOY [With a blind movement of her hand.]
Oh, Mother!

[**MRS GWYN** half turns away.]

Mother—won't you? Let's tell Uncle Tom and go away from him?

MRS GWYN
If you were not, a child, Joy, you wouldn't say such things.

JOY [Eagerly.]

I'm not a child, I'm—I'm a woman. I am.

MRS GWYN
No! You—are—not a woman, Joy.

[She sees **JOY** throw up her arms as though warding off a blow, and turning finds that **LEVER** is standing in the opening of the wall.]

LEVER [Looking from face to face.]
What's the matter? [There is no answer.] What is it, Joy?

JOY [Passionately.]
I heard you, I don't care who knows. I'd listen again.

LEVER [Impassively.]
Ah! and what did I say that was so very dreadful?

JOY
You're a—a—you 're a—coward!

MRS GWYN [With a sort of groan.]
Joy!

LEVER [Stepping up to **JOY**, and standing with his hands behind him— in a low voice.]
Now hit me in the face—hit me—hit me as hard as you can. Go on, Joy, it'll do you good.

[**JOY** raises her clenched hand, but drops it, and hides her face.

Why don't you? I'm not pretending!

[**JOY** makes no sign.]

Come, joy; you'll make yourself ill, and that won't help, will it?

[But **JOY** still makes no sign.]

[With determination.] What's the matter? now come—tell me!

JOY [In a stifled, sullen voice.]
Will you leave my mother alone?

MRS GWYN
Oh! my dear Joy, don't be silly!

JOY [Wincing; then with sudden passion.]
I defy you—I defy you!

[She rushes from their sight.]

MRS GWYN [With a movement of distress.]
Oh!

LEVER [Turning to **MRS GWYN** with a protecting gesture.]
Never mind, dear! It'll be—it'll be all right!

[But the expression of his face is not the expression of his words.]

ACT III

It is evening; a full yellow moon is shining through the branches of the hollow tree. The Chinese lanterns are alight. There is dancing in the house; the music sounds now loud, now soft. **MISS BEECH** is sitting on the rustic seat in a black bunchy evening dress, whose inconspicuous opening is inlaid with white. She slowly fans herself.

DICK comes from the house in evening dress. He does not see **MISS BEECH**.

DICK
Curse!

[A short silence.

Curse!

MISS BEECH
Poor young man!

DICK [With a start.]
Well, Peachey, I can't help it

[He fumbles off his gloves.

MISS BEECH
Did you ever know any one that could?

DICK [Earnestly.]
It's such awfully hard lines on Joy. I can't get her out of my head, lying there with that beastly headache while everybody's jigging round.

MISS BEECH
Oh! you don't mind about yourself—noble young man!

DICK
I should be a brute if I did n't mind more for her.

MISS BEECH
So you think it's a headache, do you?

DICK
Did n't you hear what Mrs. Gwyn said at dinner about the sun? [With inspiration.] I say, Peachey, could n't you—could n't you just go up and give her a message from me, and find out if there 's anything she wants, and say how brutal it is that she 's seedy; it would be most awfully decent of you. And tell her the dancing's no good without her. Do, Peachey, now do! Ah! and look here!

[He dives into the hollow of the tree, and brings from out of it a pail of water in which are placed two bottles of champagne, and some yellow irises—he takes the irises.

You might give her these. I got them specially for her, and I have n't had a chance.

MISS BEECH [Lifting a bottle.]
What 's this?

DICK
Fizz. The Colonel brought it from the George. It 's for supper; he put it in here because of—[Smiling faintly]—Mrs. Hope, I think. Peachey, do take her those irises.

MISS. BEECH
D' you think they'll do her any good?

DICK [Crestfallen.]
I thought she'd like—I don't want to worry her—you might try.

[**MISS BEECH** shakes her head.]

Why not?

MISS BEECH
The poor little creature won't let me in.

DICK
You've been up then!

MISS BEECH [Sharply.]
Of course I've been up. I've not got a stone for my heart, young man!

DICK
All right! I suppose I shall just have to get along somehow.

MISS BEECH [With devilry.]
That's what we've all got to do.

DICK [Gloomily.]
But this is too brutal for anything!

MISS BEECH
Worse than ever happened to any one!

DICK
I swear I'm not thinking of myself.

MISS BEECH
Did y' ever know anybody that swore they were?

DICK
Oh! shut up!

MISS BEECH
You'd better go in and get yourself a partner.

DICK [With pale desperation.]
Look here, Peachey, I simply loathe all those girls.

MISS BEECH
Ah-h! [Ironically.] Poor lot, are n't they?

DICK
All right; chaff away, it's good fun, isn't it? It makes me sick to dance when Joy's lying there. Her last night, too!

MISS BEECH [Sidling to him.]
You're a good young man, and you 've got a good heart.

[She takes his hand, and puts it to her cheek.]

DICK
Peachey—I say, Peachey d' you think there 's—I mean d' you think there'll ever be any chance for me?

MISS BEECH
I thought that was coming! I don't approve of your making love at your time of life; don't you think I 'm going to encourage you.

DICK
But I shall be of age in a year; my money's my own, it's not as if I had to ask any one's leave; and I mean, I do know my own mind.

MISS BEECH
Of course you do. Nobody else would at your age, but you do.

DICK
I would n't ask her to promise, it would n't be fair when she 's so young, but I do want her to know that I shall never change.

MISS BEECH
And suppose—only suppose—she's fond of you, and says she'll never change.

DICK
Oh! Peachey! D' you think there's a chance of that—do you?

MISS BEECH
A-h-h!

DICK
I wouldn't let her bind herself, I swear I wouldn't. [Solemnly.] I'm not such a selfish brute as you seem to think.

MISS BEECH [Sidling close to him and in a violent whisper.]
Well— have a go!

DICK
Really? You are a brick, Peachey!

[He kisses her.]

MISS BEECH [Yielding pleasurably; then remembering her principles.] Don't you ever say I said so! You're too young, both of you.

DICK
But it is exceptional—I mean in my case, is n't it?

[The **COLONEL** and **MRS GWYN** are coming down the lawn.]

MISS BEECH
Oh! very!

[She sits beneath the tree and fans herself.]

COLONEL
The girls are all sitting out, Dick! I've been obliged to dance myself. Phew!

[He mops his brow.]

[**DICK** swinging round goes rushing off towards the house.]

[Looking after him.] Hallo! What's the matter with him? Cooling your heels, Peachey? By George! it's hot. Fancy the poor devils in London on a night like this, what?

[He sees the moon.]

It's a full moon. You're lucky to be down here, Molly.

MRS GWYN [In a low voice.]
Very!

MISS BEECH
Oh! so you think she's lucky, do you?

COLONEL [Expanding his nostrils.]
Delicious scent to-night! Hay and roses—delicious.

[He seats himself between them.]

A shame that poor child has knocked up like this. Don't think it was the sun myself—more likely neuralgic—she 's subject to neuralgia, Molly.

MRS GWYN [Motionless.]
I know.

COLONEL
Got too excited about your coming. I told Nell not to keep worrying her about her frock, and this is the result. But your Aunt —you know—she can't let a thing alone!

MISS BEECH
Ah! 't isn't neuralgia.

[**MRS GWYN** looks at her quickly and averts her eyes.

COLONEL
Excitable little thing. You don't understand her, Peachey.

MISS BEECH
Don't I?

COLONEL
She's all affection. Eh, Molly? I remember what I was like at her age, a poor affectionate little rat, and now look at me!

MISS BEECH [Fanning herself.]
I see you.

COLONEL [A little sadly.]
We forget what we were like when we were young. She's been looking forward to to-night ever since you wrote; and now to have to go to bed and miss the dancing. Too bad!

MRS GWYN
Don't, Uncle Tom!

COLONEL [Patting her hand.]

There, there, old girl, don't think about it. She'll be all right tomorrow.

MISS BEECH
If I were her mother I'd soon have her up.

COLONEL
Have her up with that headache! What are you talking about, Peachey?

MISS BEECH
I know a remedy.

COLONEL
Well, out with it.

MISS BEECH
Oh! Molly knows it too!

MRS GWYN [Staring at the ground.]
It's easy to advise.

COLONEL [Fidgetting.]
Well, if you're thinking of morphia for her, don't have anything to do with it. I've always set my face against morphia; the only time I took it was in Burmah. I'd raging neuralgia for two days. I went to our old doctor, and I made him give me some. "Look here, doctor," I said, "I hate the idea of morphia, I 've never taken it, and I never want to."

MISS BEECH [Looking at **MRS GWYN**.]
When a tooth hurts, you should have it out. It 's only puttin' off the evil day.

COLONEL
You say that because it was n't your own.

MISS BEECH
Well, it was hollow, and you broke your principles!

COLONEL
Hollow yourself, Peachey; you're as bad as any one!

MISS BEECH [With devilry.]
Well, I know that!

[She turns to **MRS GWYN**.]

He should have had it out! Shouldn't he, Molly?

MRS GWYN
I—don't—judge for other people.

[She gets up suddenly, as though deprived of air.]

COLONEL [Alarmed.]
Hallo, Molly! Are n't you feeling the thing, old girl?

MISS BEECH
Let her get some air, poor creature!

COLONEL [Who follows anxiously.]
Your Aunt's got some first-rate sal volatile.

MRS GWYN
It's all right, Uncle Tom. I felt giddy, it's nothing, now.

COLONEL
That's the dancing.

[He taps his forehead.]

I know what it is when you're not used to it.

MRS GWYN [With a sudden bitter outburst.]
I suppose you think I 'm a very bad mother to be amusing myself while joy's suffering.

COLONEL
My dear girl, whatever put such a thought into your head? We all know if there were anything you could do, you'd do it at once, would n't she, Peachey?

[**MISS BEECH** turns a slow look on **MRS GWYN**.

MRS GWYN
Ah! you see, Peachey knows me better.

COLONEL [Following up his thoughts.]
I always think women are wonderful. There's your Aunt, she's very funny, but if there's anything the matter with me, she'll sit up all night; but when she's ill herself, and you try to do anything for her, out she raps at once.

MRS GWYN [In a low voice.]
There's always one that a woman will do anything for.

COLONEL
Exactly what I say. With your Aunt it's me, and by George! Molly, sometimes I wish it was n't.

MISS BEECH [With meaning.]
But is it ever for another woman!

COLONEL

You old cynic! D' you mean to say Joy wouldn't do anything on earth for her Mother, or Molly for Joy? You don't know human nature. What a wonderful night! Have n't seen such a moon for years, she's like a great, great lamp!

[MRS GWYN hiding from MISS BEECH'S eyes, rises and slips her arm through his; they stand together looking at the moon.

Don't like these Chinese lanterns, with that moon-tawdry! eh! By Jove, Molly, I sometimes think we humans are a rubbishy lot—each of us talking and thinking of nothing but our own petty little affairs; and when you see a great thing like that up there—[Sighs.] But there's your Aunt, if I were to say a thing like that to her she 'd— she'd think me a lunatic; and yet, you know, she 's a very good woman.

MRS GWYN [Half clinging to him.]
Do you think me very selfish, Uncle Tom?

COLONEL
My dear—what a fancy! Think you selfish—of course I don't; why should I?

MRS GWYN [Dully.]
I don't know.

COLONEL [Changing the subject nervously.]
I like your friend, Lever, Molly. He came to me before dinner quite distressed about your Aunt, beggin' me not to take those shares. She 'll be the first to worry me, but he made such a point of it, poor chap—in the end I was obliged to say I wouldn't. I thought it showed very' nice feeling. [Ruefully.] It's a pretty tight fit to make two ends meet on my income—I've missed a good thing, all owing to your Aunt. [Dropping his voice.] I don't mind telling you, Molly, I think they've got a much finer mine there than they've any idea of.

[MRS GWYN gives way to laughter that is very near to sobs.]

[With dignity.] I can't see what there is to laugh at.

MRS GWYN
I don't know what's the matter with me this evening.

MISS BEECH [In a low voice.]
I do.

COLONEL
There, there! Give me a kiss, old girl!

[He kisses her on the brow.

Why, your forehead's as hot as fire. I know—I know-you 're fretting about Joy. Never mind—come!

[He draws her hand beneath his arm.

Let's go and have a look at the moon on the river. We all get upset at times; eh!

[Lifting his hand as if he had been stung.

Why, you 're not crying, Molly! I say! Don't do that, old girl, it makes me wretched. Look here, Peachey.

[Holding out the hand on which the tear has dropped.]

This is dreadful!

MRS GWYN [With a violent effort.]
It's all right, Uncle Tom!

[**MISS BEECH** wipes her own eyes stealthily. From the house is heard the voice of **MRS HOPE**, calling "Tom."

MISS BEECH
Some one calling you.

COLONEL
There, there, my dear, you just stay here, and cool yourself—I 'll come back—shan't be a minute.

[He turns to go.

[**MRS HOPE'S** voice sounds nearer.]

[Turning back.] And Molly, old girl, don't you mind anything I said. I don't remember what it was—it must have been something, I suppose.

[He hastily retreats.

MRS GWYN [In a fierce low voice.]
Why do you torture me?

MISS BEECH [Sadly.]
I don't want to torture you.

MRS GWYN
But you do. D' you think I haven't seen this coming—all these weeks. I knew she must find out some time! But even a day counts—

MISS BEECH
I don't understand why you brought him down here.

MRS GWYN [After staring at her, bitterly.]

When day after day and night after night you've thought of nothing but how to keep them both, you might a little want to prove that it was possible, mightn't you? But you don't understand—how should you? You've never been a mother! [And fiercely.] You've never had a lov—

[**MISS BEECH** raises her face-it is all puckered.]

MRS GWYN [Impulsively.]
Oh, I did n't mean that, Peachey!

MISS BEECH
All right, my dear.

MRS GWYN
I'm so dragged in two!

[She sinks into a chair.

I knew it must come.

MISS BEECH
Does she know everything, Molly?

MRS GWYN
She guesses.

MISS BEECH [Mournfully.]
It's either him or her then, my dear; one or the other you 'll have to give up.

MRS GWYN [Motionless.]
Life's very hard on women!

MISS BEECH
Life's only just beginning for that child, Molly.

MRS GWYN
You don't care if it ends for me!

MISS BEECH
Is it as bad as that?

MRS GWYN
Yes.

MISS BEECH
[Rocking hey body.] Poor things! Poor things!

MRS GWYN
Are you still fond of me?

MISS BEECH
Yes, yes, my dear, of course I am.

MRS GWYN
In spite of my-wickedness?

[She laughs.

MISS BEECH
Who am I to tell what's wicked and what is n't? God knows you're both like daughters to me!

MRS GWYN [Abruptly.]
I can't.

MISS BEECH
Molly.

MRS GWYN
You don't know what you're asking.

MISS BEECH
If I could save you suffering, my dear, I would. I hate suffering, if it 's only a fly, I hate it.

MRS GWYN [Turning away from her.]
Life is n't fair. Peachey, go in and leave me alone.

[She leans back motionless.]

[**MISS BEECH** gets off her seat, and stroking **MRS GWYN'S** arm in passing goes silently away. In the opening of the wall she meets **LEVER** who is looking for his partner. They make way for each other.

LEVER [Going up to **MRS GWYN**—gravely.]
The next is our dance, Molly.

MRS GWYN [Unmoving.]
Let's sit it out here, then.

[**LEVER** sits down.

LEVER
I've made it all right with your Uncle.

MRS GWYN [Dully.]
Oh?

LEVER
I spoke to him about the shares before dinner.

MRS GWYN
Yes, he told me, thank you.

LEVER
There 's nothing to worry over, dear.

MRS GWYN [Passionately.]
What does it matter about the wretched shares now? I 'm stifling.

[She throws her scarf off.

LEVER
I don't understand what you mean by "now."

MRS GWYN
Don't you?

LEVER
We were n't—Joy can't know—why should she? I don't believe for a minute—

MRS GWYN
Because you don't want to.

LEVER
Do you mean she does?

MRS GWYN
Her heart knows.

[**LEVER** makes a movement of discomfiture; suddenly **MRS GWYN** looks at him as though to read his soul.]

I seem to bring you nothing but worry, Maurice. Are you tired of me?

LEVER [Meeting her eyes.]
No, I am not.

MRS GWYN
Ah, but would you tell me if you were?

LEVER [Softly.]
Sufficient unto the day is the evil thereof.

[**MRS GWYN** struggles to look at him, then covers her face with her hands.

MRS GWYN
If I were to give you up, you'd forget me in a month.

LEVER
Why do you say such things?

MRS GWYN
If only I could believe I was necessary to you!

LEVER
[Forcing the fervour of his voice.] But you are!

MRS GWYN
Am I? [With the ghost of a smile.] Midsummer day!

[She gives a laugh that breaks into a sob.]

[The music o f a waltz sounds from the house.

LEVER
For God's sake, don't, Molly—I don't believe in going to meet trouble.

MRS GWYN
It's staring me in the face.

LEVER
Let the future take care of itself!

[**MRS GWYN** has turned away her face, covering it with her hands.

Don't, Molly!

[Trying to pull her hands away.]

Don't!

MRS GWYN
Oh! what shall I do?

[There is a silence; the music of the waltz sounds louder from the house.

MRS GWYN [Starting up.]
Listen! One can't sit it out and dance it too. Which is it to be, Maurice, dancing—or sitting out? It must be one or the other, must n't it?

LEVER
Molly! Molly!

MRS GWYN
Ah, my dear!

[Standing away from him as though to show herself.

How long shall I keep you? This is all that 's left of me. It 's time I joined the wallflowers. [Smiling faintly.] It's time I played the mother, is n't it? [In a whisper.] It'll be all sitting out then.

LEVER
Don't! Let's go and dance, it'll do you good.

[He puts his hands on her arms, and in a gust of passion kisses her lips and throat.

MRS GWYN
I can't give you up—I can't. Love me, oh! love me!

[For a moment they stand so; then, with sudden remembrance of where they are, they move apart.

LEVER
Are you all right now, darling?

MRS GWYN [Trying to smile.]
Yes, dear—quite.

LEVER
Then let 's go, and dance.

[They go.

[For a few seconds the hollow tree stands alone; then from the house **ROSE** comes and enters it. She takes out a bottle of champagne, wipes it, and carries it away; but seeing **MRS GWYN'S** scarf lying across the chair, she fingers it, and stops, listening to the waltz. Suddenly draping it round her shoulders, she seizes the bottle of champagne, and waltzes with abandon to the music, as though avenging a long starvation of her instincts. Thus dancing, she is surprised by **DICK**, who has come to smoke a cigarette and think, at the spot where he was told to "have a go." **ROSE**, startled, stops and hugs the bottle.

DICK
It's not claret, Rose, I should n't warm it.

[**ROSE**, taking off the scarf, replaces it on the chair; then with the half-warmed bottle, she retreats. **DICK**, in the swing, sits thinking of his fate. Suddenly from behind the hollow tree he sees Joy darting forward in her day dress with her hair about her neck, and her skirt all torn. As he springs towards her, she turns at bay.

DICK
Joy!

JOY
I want Uncle Tom.

DICK [In consternation.]
But ought you to have got up—I thought you were ill in bed; oughtn't you to be lying down?

JOY
If have n't been in bed. Where's Uncle Tom?

DICK
But where have you been?-your dress is all torn. Look!

[He touches the torn skirt.

JOY [Tearing it away.]
In the fields. Where's Uncle Tom?

DICK
Are n't you really ill then?

[**JOY** shakes her head.

DICK [showing her the irises.]
Look at these. They were the best I could get.

JOY
Don't! I want Uncle Tom!

DICK
Won't you take them?

JOY
I 've got something else to do.

DICK [With sudden resolution.]
What do you want the Colonel for?

JOY
I want him.

DICK
Alone?

JOY
Yes.

DICK
Joy, what is the matter?

JOY
I 've got something to tell him.

DICK
What? [With sudden inspiration.] Is it about Lever?

JOY [In a low voice.]
The mine.

DICK
The mine?

JOY
It 's not—not a proper one.

DICK
How do you mean, Joy?

JOY
I overheard. I don't care, I listened. I would n't if it had been anybody else, but I hate him.

DICK [Gravely.]
What did you hear?

JOY
He 's keeping back something Uncle Tom ought to know.

DICK
Are you sure?

[**JOY** makes a rush to pass him.

DICK [Barring the way.]
No, wait a minute—you must! Was it something that really matters?—I don't want to know what.

JOY
Yes, it was.

DICK
What a beastly thing—are you quite certain, Joy?

JOY [Between her teeth.]
Yes.

DICK
Then you must tell him, of course, even if you did overhear. You can't stand by and see the Colonel swindled. Whom was he talking to?

JOY
I won't tell you.

DICK [Taking her wrist.]
Was it was it your Mother?

[**JOY** bends her head.]

But if it was your Mother, why does n't she—

JOY
Let me go!

DICK [Still holding her.]
I mean I can't see what—

JOY [Passionately.]
Let me go!

DICK [Releasing her.]
I'm thinking of your Mother, Joy. She would never—

JOY [Covering her face.]
That man!

DICK
But joy, just think! There must be some mistake. It 's so queer—it 's quite impossible!

JOY
He won't let her.

DICK
Won't let her—won't let her? But [Stopping dead, and in a very different voice.] Oh!

JOY [Passionately.]
Why d' you look at me like that? Why can't you speak?

[She waits for him to speak, but he does not.

I'm going to show what he is, so that Mother shan't speak to him again. I can—can't I—if I tell Uncle Tom?—can't I—?

DICK
But Joy—if your Mother knows a thing like—that—

JOY
She wanted to tell—she begged him—and he would n't.

DICK
But, joy, dear, it means—

JOY
I hate him, I want to make her hate him, and I will.

DICK
But, Joy, dear, don't you see—if your Mother knows a thing like that, and does n't speak of it, it means that she—it means that you can't make her hate him—it means—If it were anybody else— but, well, you can't give your own Mother away!

JOY
How dare you! How dare you!

[Turning to the hollow tree.

It is n't true—Oh! it is n't true!

DICK [In deep distress.]
Joy, dear, I never meant, I didn't really!

[He tries to pull her hands down from her face.

JOY [Suddenly.]
Oh! go away, go away!

[**MRS GWYN** is seen coming back. **JOY** springs into the tree. **DICK** quickly steals away. **MRS GWYN** goes up to the chair and takes the scarf that she has come for, and is going again when **JOY** steals out to her.

Mother!

[**MRS GWYN** stands looking at her with her teeth set on her lower lip.

Oh! Mother, it is n't true?

MRS GWYN [Very still.]
What is n't true?

JOY
That you and he are—

[Searching her **MOTHER'S** face, which is deadly still. In a whisper.

Then it is true. Oh!

MRS GWYN
That's enough, Joy! What I am is my affair—not yours— do you understand?

JOY [Low and fierce.]
Yes, I do.

MRS GWYN
You don't. You're only a child.

JOY [Passionately.]
I understand that you've hurt

[She stops.]

MRS GWYN
Do you mean your Father?

JOY [Bowing her head.]
Yes, and—and me.

[She covers her face.

I'm—I'm ashamed.

MRS GWYN
I brought you into the world, and you say that to me? Have I been a bad mother to you?

JOY [In a smothered voice.]
Oh! Mother!

MRS GWYN
Ashamed? Am I to live all my life like a dead woman because you're ashamed? Am I to live like the dead because you 're a child that knows nothing of life? Listen, Joy, you 'd better understand this once for all. Your Father has no right over me and he knows it. We 've been hateful to each other for years. Can you understand that? Don't cover your face like a child—look at me.

[**JOY** drops her hands, and lifts her face. **MRS GWYN** looks back at her, her lips are quivering; she goes on speaking with stammering rapidity.

D' you think—because I suffered when you were born and because I 've suffered since with every ache you ever had, that that gives you the right to dictate to me now? [In a dead voice.] I've been unhappy enough and I shall be unhappy enough in the time to come.

[Meeting the hard wonder in **JOY'S** face.

Oh! you untouched things, you're as hard and cold as iron!

JOY
I would do anything for you, Mother.

MRS GWYN
Except—let me live, Joy. That's the only thing you won't do for me, I quite understand.

JOY

Oh! Mother, you don't understand—I want you so; and I seem to be nothing to you now.

MRS GWYN

Nothing to me?

[She smiles.

JOY

Mother, darling, if you're so unhappy let's forget it all, let's go away and I 'll be everything to you, I promise.

MRS GWYN [With the ghost of a laugh.]

Ah, Joy!

JOY

I would try so hard.

MRS GWYN [With the same quivering smile.]

My darling, I know you would, until you fell in love yourself.

JOY

Oh, Mother, I wouldn't, I never would, I swear it.

MRS GWYN

There has never been a woman, joy, that did not fall in love.

JOY [In a despairing whisper.]

But it 's wrong of you it's wicked!

MRS GWYN

If it's wicked, I shall pay for it, not you!

JOY

But I want to save you, Mother!

MRS GWYN

Save me?

[Breaking into laughter.]

JOY

I can't bear it that you—if you 'll only—I'll never leave you. You think I don't know what I 'm saying, but I do, because even now I—I half love somebody. Oh, Mother! [Pressing her breast.] I feel—I feel so awful—as if everybody knew.

MRS GWYN

You think I'm a monster to hurt you. Ah! yes! You'll understand better some day.

JOY [In a sudden outburst of excited fear.]
I won't believe it— I—I—can't—you're deserting me, Mother.

MRS GWYN
Oh, you untouched things! You—

[**JOY** looks up suddenly, sees her face, and sinks down on her knees.

JOY
Mother—it 's for me!

MRS GWYN
Ask for my life, Joy—don't be afraid.

[**JOY** turns her face away. **MRS GWYN** bends suddenly and touches her daughter's hair; **JOY** shrinks from that touch.

[Recoiling as though she had been stung.] I forgot—I 'm deserting you.

[And swiftly without looking back she goes away. Joy, left alone under the hollow tree, crouches lower, and her shoulders shake. Here **DICK** finds her, when he hears no longer any sound of voices. He falls on his knees beside her.

DICK
Oh! Joy; dear, don't cry. It's so dreadful to see you! I 'd do anything not to see you cry! Say something.

[**JOY** is still for a moment, then the shaking of the shoulders begins again.

Joy, darling! It's so awful, you 'll make yourself ill, and it is n't worth it, really. I 'd do anything to save you pain—won't you stop just for a minute?

[**JOY** is still again.

Nothing in the world 's worth your crying, Joy. Give me just a little look!

JOY [Looking; in a smothered voice.]
Don't!

DICK
You do look so sweet! Oh, Joy, I'll comfort you, I'll take it all on myself. I know all about it.

[**JOY** gives a sobbing laugh.

I do. I 've had trouble too, I swear I have. It gets better, it does really.

JOY
You don't know—it's—it's—

DICK
Don't think about it! No, no, no! I know exactly what it's like. [He strokes her arm.]

JOY [Shrinking, in a whisper.]
You mustn't.

[The music of a waltz is heard again.

DICK
Look here, joy! It's no good, we must talk it over calmly.

JOY
You don't see! It's the—it 's the disgrace—

DICK
Oh! as to disgrace—she's your Mother, whatever she does; I'd like to see anybody say anything about her—[viciously]—I'd punch his head.

JOY [Gulping her tears.]
That does n't help.

DICK
But if she doesn't love your Father—

JOY
But she's married to him!

DICK [Hastily.]
Yes, of course, I know, marriage is awfully important; but a man understands these things.

[**JOY** looks at him. Seeing the impression he has made, he tries again.

I mean, he understands better than a woman. I've often argued about moral questions with men up at Oxford.

JOY [Catching at a straw.]
But there's nothing to argue about.

DICK [Hastily.]
Of course, I believe in morals.

[They stare solemnly at each other.

DICK
Some men don't. But I can't help seeing marriage is awfully important.

JOY [Solemnly.]

It's sacred.

DICK
Yes, I know, but there must be exceptions, Joy.

JOY [Losing herself a little in the stress of this discussion.]
How can there be exceptions if a thing 's sacred?

DICK [Earnestly.]
All rules have exceptions; that's true, you know; it's a proverb.

JOY
It can't be true about marriage—how can it when—?

DICK [With intense earnestness.]
But look here, Joy, I know a really clever man—an author. He says that if marriage is a failure people ought to be perfectly free; it isn't everybody who believes that marriage is everything. Of course, I believe it 's sacred, but if it's a failure, I do think it seems awful—don't you?

JOY
I don't know—yes—if—[Suddenly] But it's my own Mother!

DICK [Gravely.]
I know, of course. I can't expect you to see it in your own case like this. [With desperation.] But look here, Joy, this'll show you! If a person loves a person, they have to decide, have n't they? Well, then, you see, that 's what your Mother's done.

JOY
But that does n't show me anything!

DICK
But it does. The thing is to look at it as if it was n't yourself. If it had been you and me in love, Joy, and it was wrong, like them, of course [ruefully] I know you'd have decided right. [Fiercely.] But I swear I should have decided wrong. [Triumphantly.] That 's why I feel I understand your Mother.

JOY [Brushing her sleeve across her eyes.]
Oh, Dick, you are so sweet—and—and—funny!

DICK [Sliding his arm about her.]
I love you, Joy, that 's why, and I 'll love you till you don't feel it any more. I will. I'll love you all day and every day; you shan't miss anything, I swear it. It 's such a beautiful night—it 's on purpose. Look'

[**JOY** looks; he looks at her.

But it 's not so beautiful as you.

JOY [Bending her head.]
You mustn't. I don't know—what's coming?

DICK [Sidling closer.]
Are n't your knees tired, darling? I—I can't get near you properly.

JOY [With a sob.]
Oh! Dick, you are a funny—comfort!

DICK
We'll stick together, Joy, always; nothing'll matter then.

[They struggle to their feet-the waltz sounds louder.

You're missing it all! I can't bear you to miss the dancing. It seems so queer! Couldn't we? Just a little turn?

JOY
No, no?

DICK
Oh! try!

[He takes her gently by the waist, she shrinks back.

JOY [Brokenly.]
No-no! Oh! Dick-to-morrow 'll be so awful.

DICK
To-morrow shan't hurt you, Joy; nothing shall ever hurt you again.

[She looks at him, and her face changes; suddenly she buries it against his shoulder.

[They stand so just a moment in the moon light; then turning to the river move slowly out of sight. Again the hollow tree is left alone. The music of the waltz has stopped. The voices of **MISS BEECH** and the **COLONEL** are heard approaching from the house. They appear in the opening of the wall. The **COLONEL** carries a pair of field glasses with which to look at the Moon.

COLONEL
Charming to see Molly dance with Lever, their steps go so well together! I can always tell when a woman's enjoying herself, Peachey.

MISS BEECH [Sharply.]
Can you? You're very clever.

COLONEL
Wonderful, that moon! I'm going to have a look at her! Splendid glasses these, Peachy [he screws them out], not a better pair in England. I remember in Burmah with these glasses I used to be able to tell a man from a woman at two miles and a quarter. And that's no joke, I can tell you.

[But on his way to the moon, he has taken a survey of the earth to the right along the river. In a low but excited voice.

COLONEL
I say, I say—is it one of the maids—the baggage! Why! It's Dick! By George, she's got her hair down, Peachey! It's Joy!

[**MISS BEECH** goes to look. He makes as though to hand the glasses to her, but puts them to his own eyes instead— excitedly.

COLONEL
It is! What about her headache? By George, they're kissing. I say, Peachey! I shall have to tell Nell!

MISS BEECH
Are you sure they're kissing? Well, that's some comfort.

COLONEL
They're at the stile now. Oughtn't I to stop them, eh? [He stands on tiptoe.] We must n't spy on them, dash it all.

[He drops the glasses.

COLONEL
They're out of sight now.

MISS BEECH [To herself.]
He said he wouldn't let her.

COLONEL
What! have you been encouraging them!

MISS BEECH
Don't be in such a hurry!

[She moves towards the hollow tree.

COLONEL [Abstractedly.]
By George, Peachey, to think that Nell and I were once—Poor Nell! I remember just such a night as this—

[He stops, and stares before him, sighing.

MISS BEECH [Impressively.]
It's a comfort she's got that good young man. She's found out that her mother and this Mr. Lever are—you know.

COLONEL [Losing all traces of his fussiness, and drawing himself up as though he were on parade.]
You tell me that my niece?

MISS BEECH
Out of her own mouth!

COLONEL [Bowing his head.]
I never would have believed she'd have forgotten herself.

MISS BEECH [Very solemnly.]
Ah, my dear! We're all the same; we're all as hollow as that tree! When it's ourselves it's always a special case!

[The **COLONEL** makes a movement of distress, and **MISS BEECH** goes to him.

Don't you take it so to heart, my dear!

[A silence.

COLONEL [Shaking his head.]
I couldn't have believed Molly would forget that child.

MISS BEECH [Sadly.]
They must go their own ways, poor things! She can't put herself in the child's place, and the child can't put herself in Molly's. A woman and a girl—there's the tree of life between them!

COLONEL [Staring into the tree to see indeed if that were the tree alluded to.]
It's a grief to me, Peachey, it's a grief!

[He sinks into a chair, stroking his long moustaches. Then to avenge his hurt.]

COLONEL
Shan't tell Nell—dashed if I do anything to make the trouble worse!

MISS BEECH [Nodding.]
There's suffering enough, without adding to it with our trumpery judgments! If only things would last between them!

COLONEL [Fiercely.]
Last! By George, they'd better—

[He stops, and looking up with a queer sorry look.]

COLONEL
I say, Peachey Life's very funny!

MISS BEECH
Men and women are! [Touching his forehead tenderly.] There, there—take care of your poor, dear head! Tsst! The blessed innocents!

[She pulls the **COLONEL'S** sleeve. They slip away towards the house, as **JOY** and **DICK** come back. They are still linked together, and stop by the hollow tree.

JOY [In a whisper.]
Dick, is love always like this?

DICK [Putting his arms around her, with conviction.]
It's never been like this before. It's you and me!

[He kisses her on the lips.

John Galsworthy – A Short Biography

John Galsworthy, eldest son of John Galsworthy (1817-1904), a solicitor and company director of Old Jewry, London, and Blanche Bailey (1835-1915), daughter of Charles Bartleet, a needlemaker in Redditch. His father's ancestors originated in Wembury, near Plymouth in England, and Galsworthy, for whom family origins were of significant importance, maintained a close connection with Devon. His more immediate family were considerably wealthy and well established in the shipping industry, and owned a fine estate in Kingston-upon-Thames called Parkfield, where Galsworthy was born on the 14th August 1867. At the age of nine he began education at Saugeen, a Bournemouth preparatory school, before starting at Harrow school in 1881 where he remained until 1886, distinguishing himself as an athlete.

His education at Harrow being successful enough to gain him entrance to Oxford, he began at New College to read law and gained a second-class degree with honours in 1889. Following Lincoln's Inn he was called to the bar in 1890. Despite this recognition he realised that he was not keen to actually begin practising law and so he resolved instead to look after the family's shipping business while specialising himself in Marine Law. This decision saw him take to the seas to destinations such as Vancouver, Island and South AFrica, though it was at the age of twenty-five on one particular journey to Australia, motivated by an (unfulfilled) intention to meet Robert Louis Stevenson on Samoa that he would being to realise fully his literary interests: though he was not considering becoming a writer at this time, his enjoyment of literature was enough to encourage an attempt at meeting a great writer and eventually enabled one of the most significant encounters of his life. He made the journey with his friend Edward Sanderson and, though he missed Stevenson, he met Joseph Conrad, a fellow future author famed for his novels which were often nautically themed. At the time Conrad was the first mate of the sailing-ship Torrens moored in the harbour of Adelaide, Australia; still very much focused on his ship-borne career, he was yet to begin his writing in earnest.

Indeed, though neither knew at the time, both Conrad and Galsworthy were at similar junctures in their lives, their time spent as sea acting as a transitional period during which each found their literary calling. It is perhaps owing to this unknown common ground that they became close friends. During his time on the Torrens Galsworthy recorded several details, offering a frank and valuable characterisation of Conrad while also illuminating his own experiences as a student of Marine Law.

> "I supposed to be studying navigation for the Admiralty Bar, would every day work
> out the position of the ship with the captain. On one side of the saloon table we

would sit and check our observations with those of Conrad, who from the other side of the table would look at us a little quizzically."

On his return to England and the cessation of his nautical voyaging, Galsworthy began an affair with the wife of his first cousin, Major Arthur John Galsworthy. Ada Nemesis Pearson Cooper (1864-1956), the daughter of Emanuel Copper, an obstetrician from Norwich, remained married to the Major for ten years and the affair remained secret for its duration. In order to conceal the affair they took considerable pains to avoid suspicion. One such tactic was to stay in a secluded farmhouse called Wingstone in the village on Manaton on Dartmoor, in Devon. In Galsworthy's decision to choose Devon as the location for their clandestine rendezvous we see evidence of Galsworthy's affection for the place of his father's origin. It was only when, in 1905, she divorced the Major that their affair became known following their marriage on 23rd September of that year.

Galsworthy now took to writing sometime after having met Conrad and his career began in earnest when, in 1897, his first work, From the Four Winds, a volume of short stories, was published under the pseudonym John Sinjohn. He succeeded this in 1898 with Jocelyn, his first novel, and then his second in 1900, Villa Rubein. In 1901 he published a second volume of short stories, A Man of Devon, which was the last of his work to be published under pseudonym. The first of his work to be published under his own name was The Island Pharisees in 1904, a novel of social observation, seasoned with flashes of satire and propaganda. His decision to write under his own name is arguably owing to the recent death of his father, either as a mark of respect to his name or because now he was able to publish freely without incurring the possibility of paternal disappointment at his choice of career. It also marked a shift in his professionalism; he had hitherto published with small, independent publishers, but The Island Pharisees was published by Heinemann, a far more established House and one with whom he remained for the duration of his writing career.

He arguably cemented his position and maturity as a writer when, in 1906, he saw the publication of both his first major play, The Silver Box, and the novel The Man of Property. Each was published to considerable critical acclaim, and to achieve both in such a short space of time was impressive. the Silver Box concerns the imbalance in the justice system with regards to criminals of differing class by contrasting the treatment of a poor thief and a rich thief, both of whom stole silver cigarette cases but for very different reasons. The complexity of individual experience when not dealt with in public is highlighted and questioned in a bravely critical manner; despite the clear issues it raises with class and privilege, the final night was attended by the Price and Princess of Wales. The Man of Property was the first novel in the famous The Forsyte Saga, a trilogy of novels with an 'interlude' between each one, written between 1906 and 1921. Dealing with the questions of status, class and materialism, The Man of Property introduces us to the Forsyte family, particularly Soames Forsyte, who is acutely aware of his status as 'new money' and equally keen to assert himself as a wealthy man. Jealous of his wife and desperate to own things in order to confirm his wealth to those observing him, he engineers a plan to keep his wife from her friends which backfires spectacularly when, instead of cutting her off, all Soames achieves is enabling her to have an affair. This drives Soames to terrible actions with terrible consequences, which Galsworthy depicts with confidence.

Very typically Edwardian, the novel focuses on conflict between property and art, and to a certain degree much of its emotional power is drawn from Galsworthy's own life, particularly his affair with Ada. Their rendezvous in the countryside of Devon mirror the manner in which Forsyte seeks to relocate his wife and; though theirs was a much healthier relationship, there are clear similarities. By examining the fragile nature of the class system and those moving within it Galsworthy offered an important perspective on the relationships between material wealth, personal happiness and obsession, and the manner in which these change over time. His contemporaries widely regarded the publication of this novel as marking the end of Victorianism. His friend Conrad praised it as "indubitably a piece of art" and, though the notoriously risqué D.H. Lawrence lamented the novel's timidity in the face of sexuality and sensuality, he considered it potentially "a very great novel, a very great satire".

Though he continued to write both plays and novels, it was his work as a playwright for which he was most celebrated by his contemporaries. Indeed, his next novel, The Country House, seems uncharacteristically unfocused, its satirical view of those belonging to the country set comparatively unremarkable and weakly characterised, while at times the tone of satire becomes one of ironic detachment. In 1909 he published Fraternity, an exploration of of the various connections between urban society and the social classes therein, though its representation of lower-class Londoners is utterly unconvincing and ill-informed. Remaining with the subject of the landed gentry and the society surrounding it, in 1915 he published The Freelands, which does not stray far from conservative discussions of capitalism, the rural economy and their interrelationship.

His drama, however, featured a convincingly muted realism, directed at a relatively small, educated and politically-aware audience. His social agenda is prevalent here too, and is represented in a simple and static manner producing arresting instances of high drama. This talent for creating moments of captivating theatre is complimented by an instinctual sense of balance enabling his narratives to vacillate between their emotional high- and low-points, ultimately reaching conclusive equilibrium. This is particularly evident in one of his most popular plays, Strife, published in 1909 and examining the antagonists in a strike at a Cornish tin mine. In this, and in 1910's Justice, he approaches his subject with sympathy, irony and balance, which establishes a position of narrative authority while garnering the audiences trust that he is representing his characters and their motives justly. Justice condemns the use of solitary confinement in prisons, a reformist agenda which caught the liberality of his contemporary audiences along with the home secretary, Winston Churchill. Despite he was careful to disassociate himself with politics and professed himself apolitical, he and his work were nevertheless aligned with the views of the Liberal establishment. He spent much of the duration of the First World War working in a field hospital in France as an orderly having been passed over for military service.

Despite the popularity and brilliance of his work, it was only in 1920 that he had his first true commercial success with The Skin Game, a melodrama dealing with ethics, property and class. The play was adapted by Alfred Hitchcock in 1931. Galsworthy, meanwhile, had turned down a knighthood in 1918, considering his work not sufficient to be made a knight of the realm. He did, however, accept the Belgian Palmes d'Or in the following year. In 1920 he published the second novel in the Forsyte Saga, In Chancery, in which he resumes many of the themes of the first novel, focusing on the marital disharmony between Soames Forsyte and his wife. Katherine Mansfield considered it "a fascinating, brilliant book" in her review in The Atheneum. Then, in 1921, he was elected as the PEN International Literary Club's first president. The concluding novel to The Forsyte Saga, To Let was published in 1921 with a kind of peace being found between Forsyte and his now-ex wife, though he is left contemplating his losses and his greed. More ironic treatment of class confusions followed in Loyalties, bringing with it more popular success which lasted until 1926 and Escape, the last of his popular plays. Though he enjoyed popular success it was inconsistent and relatively small. His Collected Plays was published in 1929.

Over the course of time the appreciation of his work has gradually shifted from his plays to his novels, and particularly the detail and intricacy of his chronicle of English social difference, tension and pretension in The Forsyte Saga. Its success encouraged Galsworthy to revisit Soames Forsyte in a second trilogy, A Modern Comedy, which follows Soames's obsessive love of his daughter Fleur. In its three volumes, The White Monkey (1924), The Silver Spoon (1936) and Swan Song (1928) he examines the English commercial upper-middle class and its ideologies, its instinct to possess as its only way of distinguishing itself manifested in the poisonous materialism of Soames. Interestingly, this emergent social class which he so vehemently criticises is the very class from which he emerged. He witnessed first-hand its insularity, its chauvinism, its restrictive and oppressive morality, its stubborn imperialism and its materialism, and it is this experience which enables him to write so comfortably about it. Swan Song is widely considered among the best of Galsworthy's writing for the depth of its exploration of society and its heightened emotional subtlety. In 1929 he was appointed to the Order of Merit, despite having turned down a knighthood earlier. He spent his last years writing a third trilogy, End of the Chapter, beginning in 1931 with Maid in Waiting, Flowering Wilderness in 1932 and concluding with Over The River in 1933. These are significantly less coherent works and are indicative of his deteriorating health. Indeed, in 1932 he was awarded the Nobel Prize, though he was too ill to attend the ceremony.

Throughout the course of his career he received honorary degrees from the universities of St Andrews (1922), Manchester (1927), Dublin (1929), Cambridge (1930), Sheffield (1930), Oxford (1931), and Princeton (1931). In 1926 New College, Oxford, elected him as an honourary fellow. In photographs he is portrayed as handsome, fastidiously dressed and dignified. He was unusually compassionate and this saw him involved in several charitable and humane causes throughout the course of his life, including penal reforms, attacks on theatrical censorship and campaigning for animal rights. Though he spent the majority of the final seven years of his life at his home in Bury, West Sussex, it was at his home in Hampstead, London, that he died of a brain tumour on 31st January, 1933, six weeks after having been too ill to attend the ceremony in honour of his receiving the Nobel Prize. According to demands made in his will he was cremated and his ashes scattered over the South Downs from an aeroplane. Also in his will was his wish to leave cottages to several of his astonished tenants. He is memorialised in Highgate 'New' Cemetery and in the cloisters of New College, Oxford, where he was an honourary fellow.

John Galsworthy – A Concise Bibliography

From the Four Winds, 1897 (as John Sinjohn)
Jocelyn, 1898 (as John Sinjohn)
Villa Rubein, 1900 (as John Sinjohn)
A Man of Devon, 1901 (as John Sinjohn)
The Island Pharisees, 1904
The Silver Box, 1906 (his first play)
The Man of Property, 1906 – First book of The Forsyte Saga (1922)
The Country House, 1907
A Commentary, 1908
Fraternity, 1909
A Justification for the Censorship of Plays, 1909
Strife, 1909
Fraternity, 1909
Joy, 1909
Justice, 1910
A Motley, 1910

The Spirit of Punishment, 1910
Horses in Mines, 1910
The Patrician, 1911
The Little Dream, 1911
The Pigeon, 1912
The Eldest Son, 1912
Quality, 1912
Moods, Songs, and Doggerels, 1912
For Love of Beasts, 1912
The Inn of Tranquillity, 1912
The Dark Flower, 1913
The Fugitive, 1913
The Mob, 1914
The Freelands, 1915
The Little Man, 1915
A Bit o' Love, 1915
A Sheaf, 1916
The Apple Tree, 1916
The Foundations, 1917
Beyond, 1917
Five Tales, 1918
Indian Summer of a Forsyte, 1918 – First interlude of The Forsyte Saga
Saint's Progress, 1919
Addresses in America, 1912
In Chancery, 1920 – Second book of The Forsyte Saga
Awakening, 1920 – Second interlude of The Forsyte Saga
The Skin Game, 1920
To Let, 1921 – Third book of The Forsyte Saga
A Family Man, 1922
The Little Man, 1922
Loyalties, 1922
Windows, 1922
Captures, 1923
Abracadabra, 1924
The Forest, 1924
Old English, 1924
The White Monkey, 1924 – First book of A Modern Comedy (1929)
The Show, 1925
Escape, 1926
The Silver Spoon, 1926 – Second book of A Modern Comedy
Verses New and Old, 1926
Castles in Spain, 1927
A Silent Wooing, 1927 – First Interlude of A Modern Comedy
Passers By, 1927 – Second Interlude of A Modern Comedy
Swan Song, 1928 – Third book of A Modern Comedy
The Manaton Edition, 1923–26 (collection, 30 vols.)
Exiled, 1929
The Roof, 1929

On Forsyte 'Change, 1930
Two Essays on Conrad, 1930
Soames and the Flag, 1930
The Creation of Character in Literature, 1931 (The Romanes Lecture for 1931).
Maid in Waiting, 1931 – First book of End of the Chapter (1934)
Forty Poems, 1932
Flowering Wilderness, 1932 – Second book of End of the Chapter
Autobiographical Letters of Galsworthy: A Correspondence with Frank Harris, 1933
One More River (originally Over the River), 1933 – Third book of End of the Chapter
The Grove Edition, 1927–34 (collection, 27 Vols.)
Collected Poems, 1934
Punch and Go, 1935
The Life and Letters, 1935
The Winter Garden, 1935
Forsytes, Pendyces and Others, 1935
Selected Short Stories, 1935
Glimpses and Reflections, 1937
Galsworthy's Letters to Leon Lion, 1968
Letters from John Galsworthy 1900–1932, 1970
Caravan the assembled tales of John Galsworthy, New York Charles Scribner's Sons 1925

www.ingramcontent.com/pod-product-compliance
Lightning Source LLC
Chambersburg PA
CBHW060136050426
42448CB00010B/2156